Find more of my work at my blog:

www.theauthorstack.com

Find all my work at my website:

www.russellnohelty.com

Bookbub:

https://www.bookbub.com/profile/russell-nohelty

HOW TO WRITE IRRESISTIBLE BOOKS THAT READERS DEVOUR

By:
Russell Nohelty

Edited by:
Lily Luchesi

Proofread by:
Katrina Roets

Copyright © 2025 by Russell Nohelty

Published by Wannabe Press

All Rights Reserved.

This is a nonfiction work. Russell Nohelty and Wannabe Press do not guarantee any outcomes from following the advice in this book. We are not lawyers, accountants, or other specialized professionals. We take no responsibility for what happens if you take this advice. It's worked for us and many others we know. However, this is simply the accumulated experience of one man making his journey into the world. While we think it is very good advice, there is no guarantee it will work for you.

First Edition, August 2025

A BRIDGE BETWEEN STORIES AND READERS

Every story begins with a spark; a moment when an idea catches fire in a writer's mind and demands to be shared. But the journey from that initial spark to a published work that truly resonates with readers is more complex than simply putting words on a page. It requires understanding not just the craft of storytelling, but the deeper psychology of how stories connect with readers on an emotional level.

In the summer of 2024, my business partner, Monica Leonelle and I hosted a series of live calls for a course called Storyurge. This book was compiled from the transcripts of those calls, along with information from other courses I've produced over the years, and some articles from my publication, The Author Stack (www.theauthorstack.com). I've been working with authors for over fifteen years and have been growing my fiction and non-fiction career since then. I never set out to write non-fiction, but it's been a happy accident to work with so many wonderful creators and help them build their dreams.

In all that time, I've never written a craft book, and until this book I've only sparingly written about craft across my career. It was a joy to finally have a chance to dig deep into what I've thought about craft, and help you tell the most powerful stories possible readers can't help but devour.

THE POWER OF CONNECTION

Consider *Star Wars*. On the surface, it's another hero's journey about a farm boy discovering his destiny. Yet, it resonates deeply because *Star Wars* isn't just about space battles. It's about the emotional bonds between its characters. Luke's arc isn't just about defeating the Empire. It's about finding belonging after loss.

His connection to Obi-Wan gives him guidance, his friendship with Han and Leia gives him purpose, and his discovery of Darth Vader's identity later adds depth to his internal struggles.

Even iconic lines like *"May the Force be with you"* work because they aren't just catchphrases. They symbolize trust, hope, and the unseen bonds that tie people together.

Star Wars isn't just a sci-fi adventure; it's a story about connection, which is why it continues to resonate across generations.

This is the essence of what we'll explore in this book: how to create stories that don't just entertain but forge genuine connections with readers. Whether you're writing fantasy epics or contemporary romance, the principles remain the same. Your story must serve as a bridge between your creative vision and your readers' emotional needs.

Traditional writing advice often focuses on the mechanics, including plot structure, character development, and world-building. While these elements are crucial, they're only part of the equation. The most successful authors understand that every aspect of their story, from the broadest themes to the smallest details, must serve a deeper purpose.

Think about how *Game of Thrones* introduces its world. George R.R. Martin doesn't overwhelm readers with fantasy elements immediately. Instead, he begins with familiar human dynamics like family relationships, political intrigue, and personal ambition before gradually introducing more fantastical elements. This allows readers to acclimate to new elements while maintaining their connection to the story's emotional core.

As authors, we wear many hats. We are creators, crafting worlds and characters from nothing. We are psychologists, understanding the deep emotional triggers that make stories resonate. We are marketers, finding ways to connect our work with the readers who need it most. This multiplicity of roles can feel overwhelming, but it doesn't have to be.

Throughout this book, we'll explore how these different aspects of authorship can work together harmoniously. You'll learn how to:

- Create stories that hook readers from the first page and keep them invested until the last
- Understand the psychological triggers that make stories memorable and meaningful
- Build worlds that feel both fresh and familiar
- Develop marketing approaches that feel authentic rather than promotional
- Transform casual readers into passionate advocates for your work

Traditional writing advice often treats craft and marketing as separate disciplines. But in today's publishing landscape, this division no longer serves us. The same principles that make a story emotionally resonant also make it marketable. The same understanding of psychological triggers that helps us create compelling characters also helps us connect with readers effectively.

Consider how the most successful series build their audiences over time. *The Dresden Files* begins with a simple premise. It's about a wizard working as a private investigator in Chicago. But with each book, Jim Butcher deepens both the world and the emotional stakes, giving readers more reasons to invest in the story while maintaining the core elements that drew them in initially.

In the chapters ahead, we'll explore every aspect of creating stories that resonate deeply with readers. We'll examine how to develop characters that feel real enough to step off the page, craft worlds that readers want to live in, and build plots that keep them turning pages late into the night. We'll look at how to use psychological triggers effectively and ethically, creating marketing that feels like a natural extension of your storytelling rather than a separate task.

This isn't just about writing better books. It's about understanding the bridge between stories and readers, between creative vision and audience connection. It's about mastering both the art and science of storytelling in a way that serves both creator and audience.

Whether you're working on your first novel or your fiftieth, the principles in this book will help you create work that resonates more deeply and reaches more readers. The journey begins with understanding that every story is an opportunity to build a bridge between author and reader, between imagination and reality, between what is and what could be.

GETTING YOUR MINDSET RIGHT BEFORE YOU DIVE IN

Even the most brilliant concept will remain just that without the proper mental approach to see it through to completion. Perhaps the most daunting challenge any writer faces is the terror of the blank page. That pristine white expanse can feel like an accusation, a canvas too perfect to mar with our imperfect words.

This fear is particularly acute for novelists because we're tasked with creating entire worlds from nothing - a challenge most other professions never face. The solution, counterintuitive as it may seem, is to embrace imperfection.

Begin by writing anything, even if it's stream-of-consciousness rambling. The simple act of putting words on the page helps break the psychological barrier, reminding your brain that you are, in fact, a writer, simply by virtue of writing.

This ties into a broader principle: *the necessity of showing up consistently.* Studies have shown that mere exposure to something, or in this case, regular engagement with the craft, naturally builds familiarity and comfort over time. Setting concrete goals, whether they're time-based or word-count-based, creates a framework for this consistency.

The key is to make these goals non-negotiable. When you commit to not leaving your chair until you've written 250 words or edited one chapter, you're training your creative mind to respond to structure rather than waiting for inspiration.

We also have to learn to embrace "the cringe". Every writer, particularly at the beginning of their career, will experience profound discomfort when reading their own work. This is not only **normal** but actually a positive sign. It means your critical faculties are developing faster than your creative abilities can keep up.

The gap between what you can envision and what you can currently execute is what drives improvement. As you continue writing, this gap narrows, not because your standards lower, but because your skills rise to meet them.

The middle of a novel presents its own unique psychological challenges. While beginnings carry the excitement of possibility and endings promise the thrill of completion, the middle can feel like an endless slog. This "middle dread" separates the winners from the quitters in the writing world. Luckily, this feeling is universal. We've all dealt with it at some point. I've been writing for 15+ years, and I abandoned two books in the middle of last year. Understanding that every successful author has navigated this same psychological terrain can help you push through it. The key is to accept that the middle isn't supposed to feel exciting; it's where the real work happens.

When facing creative blocks, it's crucial to distinguish between two types: those born of simple resistance to the work (which require pushing through) and those that signal genuine problems with the story (which require listening to). The former is conquered through discipline and routine, while the latter might require strategic retreat and revision. The trick is developing the wisdom to know the difference, which comes only through experience.

Finally, and perhaps most importantly, successful writers understand that process is everything. ***When inspiration fails, when doubts creep in, when external pressures mount, your established process becomes your lifeline.*** It's the set of habits and practices that carry you through when motivation falters. This means developing not just writing routines, but also systems for organizing ideas, approaches to revision, and strategies for overcoming common obstacles.

The right mindset isn't about eliminating fear or doubt - it's about learning to produce quality work despite them. By accepting the inherent challenges of the creative process while maintaining steadfast dedication to craft and routine, writers can transform their relationship with the work from one of anxiety to one of purposeful engagement.

Write Irresistible Books that Readers Devour

THE ANATOMY OF HOOKY IDEAS

Every time we sit down with authors trying to figure out why their books aren't selling, we inevitably circle back to the same block. The core idea isn't hooking readers. There are lots of fixable problems in this writing life, but starting from the wrong core is the hardest to fix.

Sure, craft matters. Marketing matters. But without a concept that grabs people and refuses to let go, you're fighting an uphill battle from page one.

Here's what most writing books won't tell you: coming up with truly hooky ideas isn't just about waiting for inspiration to strike. It's a skill you can develop systematically once you understand the building blocks. We've spent years studying what makes certain stories catch fire while others fizzle out, and we're going to break down exactly what we've learned.

The process of cultivating and selecting story ideas is perhaps the most foundational skill for aspiring novelists. While many writers focus on how to generate ideas, experienced authors understand that identifying and developing the right idea is far more crucial than simply generating many concepts.

The first step in my process is counterintuitive: when you have a new idea, do nothing. Instead of immediately jumping into development, let the idea prove itself through persistence. I force the best ideas to struggle against the current until they prove they are sticky in my mind. If I keep coming back to it, then there's a good chance it will resonate with other people, too.

A compelling story concept will return to your thoughts repeatedly, demanding attention and generating continued excitement with each visit. This natural filtering process might take a week, a month, or even a year, but an idea that keeps resurfacing and maintains its appeal over time has demonstrated the first sign of promise.

Only after an idea has passed this initial test does it earn a place in my development folder. This approach prevents me from becoming overwhelmed by every passing thought and ensures you're investing time in concepts that have already shown staying power. However, even reaching your development folder doesn't guarantee an idea is ready for full execution.

The next crucial understanding is that individual ideas *rarely make a complete story on their own.* The magic often happens when you begin combining multiple concepts from your collection. A simple premise about a "skate park" might not sustain a novel by itself, but when merged with elements from other story seeds it could evolve into something more substantial and unique than any of the individual pieces.

The final and most critical test for any story idea is what we might call the "spark joy" factor. It's not enough for an idea to simply interest you. It needs to generate overwhelming enthusiasm. Ask yourself: *Are you willing to spend the next one to two years developing this story?* Can you envision yourself promoting it for five to ten years afterward? The project will become less exciting over time as you work through the challenges of development, so your initial passion needs to be strong enough to sustain you through the inevitable difficult periods.

Remember that passion is infectious. If you don't love your idea "a hundred and crazy percent," it's unlikely that readers will either. The story needs to excite you so profoundly that even when it beats you down during the writing process, your remaining enthusiasm is still sufficient to carry you through to completion.

When an idea combination passes all these tests, it's ready to take the next step. This careful cultivation and selection process helps ensure that you're investing your time and creative energy in projects with the greatest potential for success.

HIGH CONCEPT VS LOW CONCEPT

Before diving into specific techniques, we need to talk about story scale. Every story exists on a spectrum from high concept to low concept and understanding where your idea falls on this spectrum shapes everything that follows.

In movies, this distinction is obvious. When a studio shells out $200 million for a blockbuster, they want a high concept premise they can sell in a single sentence. "An astronaut gets stranded on Mars and has to science his way home." Boom. That's *The Martian*. The premise alone tells you what you're getting and why you should care.

This is what movie studios call a "four-quadrant movie". A four-quadrant film is designed to appeal to four key demographic groups: males under 25, males over 25, females under 25, and females over 25. This broad appeal is achieved not through trying to please everyone superficially, but by creating layered storytelling that works on multiple levels simultaneously.

Think of how *The Lion King* offers colorful characters and clear messages about growing up for young viewers, while exploring deeper themes of grief, legacy, and responsibility that resonate with adults. The key lies in weaving together universal experiences and emotions that transcend demographic boundaries while maintaining enough depth that different viewers can find their own meaningful connections to the story.

We tend to focus on these blockbuster movies, while ignoring the fact that some of the most successful stories of all time are actually low concept. Take *The Office*. The premise is literally just "people working at a paper company." No world-ending stakes. No dramatic hook. Just human beings existing in a mundane setting. Yet it ran for nine seasons and became a cultural touchstone because it understood exactly what it was trying to be.

The key is matching your concept level to your story's needs. We see writers constantly trying to force intimate character studies into high-concept frameworks because they think that's what sells. Or they'll take a premise that needs room to breathe and try to compress it into a quiet character piece. Either approach is like trying to fit a square peg into a round hole. It just doesn't work.

The Good Place and *Parks and Recreation* were created by the same showrunner, Michael Schur. One's high concept (woman dies and mistakenly ends up in heaven), one's low concept (local government employees try to build a park). Both were hugely successful because they understood their concept level and leaned into it.

The Good Place used its high concept premise to explore big philosophical questions about what it means to be a good person. The fantastical setting gave them room to play with huge ideas while keeping the story accessible through character relationships. Meanwhile, *Parks and Recreation* drew its strength from intimate character dynamics and small-stakes conflicts that built emotional investment over time.

Where we see a lot of writers stumble is that they assume "high concept" automatically means better. But concept level is just a tool, not a value judgment. Low concept stories can be just as compelling as high concept ones. Often more so, because they have room to dig deep into character and emotion without the pressure of constantly escalating external stakes.

Just look at the emergence of the cozy fantasy genre in the past couple of years as an example of how bigger is not always better.

That said, concept levels aren't fixed, either. Many successful series actually shift their concept level over time. *The Crown* is a perfect example. It started as a high-concept historical drama about the young Queen Elizabeth II taking the throne. Big stakes, big historical moments, big drama. But as the series progressed, it became more of a family drama that happened to be set against a historical backdrop. The concept level shifted from high to low as the series found its groove.

We see this pattern a lot on television, particularly in shows that run for multiple seasons. *The Vampire Diaries* started as a relatively straightforward teen vampire romance, which is pretty low concept for the genre. But with each season, the stakes got bigger, the mythology more complex, until they were dealing with original vampires and world-threatening supernatural events. The concept level kept rising until they actually had to reset it because they'd gone as big as they could go.

This brings us to an important point about sustainability. High concept stories often struggle with escalation because they start at such a high intensity. Where do you go after the world almost ends in book one? Low concept stories usually have more room to grow and evolve naturally. This doesn't mean one approach is better, it just means you need to plan differently depending on your concept level.

Think about your story. Is it inherently high concept or low concept? Could it work at a different concept level? Most importantly, are you trying to force it to be something it's not? Understanding your story's natural concept level helps you develop it in a way that plays to its strengths rather than fighting against its nature.

BUILDING STORIES THAT LAST

Writing a single book is challenging enough. Building a story world that can sustain multiple books while keeping readers engaged? That's a whole different game. Yet understanding story sustainability isn't just for series writers - even standalone novels need enough depth to carry readers through hundreds of pages.

The Dresden Files offers a masterclass in sustainable story building. Jim Butcher didn't launch straight into world-ending stakes. Instead, he started with something manageable: a wizard working as a private investigator in Chicago. Simple premise, easy entry point for readers. But within that premise, he planted seeds that would grow into much bigger stories. By the time readers get to the zombie T. rex charging through downtown Chicago in later books, it feels like a natural evolution rather than a desperate attempt to raise stakes.

This is where a lot of series writers stumble. They burn through their best material too quickly, leaving nowhere interesting to go. You see this especially in shows that weren't planned for long runs. Remember how *Supernatural* had a tight five-season arc planned? When it got renewed beyond that, they had to basically reinvent the show because they'd already played their biggest cards.

A great strategy to avoiding this trap lies in something called The Levitz Paradigm, named after comic editor Paul Levitz. Instead of thinking of your story as a single thread, imagine juggling multiple plot lines at different stages of development:

Your A-story drives the current book. It's your main conflict, your big emotional payoff, but while that's running, you're developing B-stories that might become future A-stories. Meanwhile, you're seeding C-stories and D-stories that could grow into bigger plots down the line. When your current A-story wraps up, you've got fully developed B-stories ready to take center stage, creating natural story progression.

Russell Nohelty

A typical novel might contain five distinct plot threads of varying importance: a primary plot (taking up about 40,000 words), a secondary plot (25,000 words), and decreasing word counts for additional subplots (20,000, 10,000, and 5,000 words respectively). Think about how *The Matrix* balances its main plot of Neo's journey with subplots involving the resistance movement, the nature of reality, and various character relationships.

Game of Thrones demonstrates this beautifully. Characters who start as minor players in early books gradually develop into major viewpoint characters. Take Davos Seaworth, for example. He begins as a supporting character, becomes a viewpoint character, and eventually carries major plot threads. This wasn't accidental. George R.R. Martin planted these characters early, giving them room to grow organically as the story expanded.

Elana Johnson takes this approach even further in her romance series. She deliberately seeds book seven's hero in book one because she knows reader engagement often drops around book seven. By planting that character early and maintaining light touches of their story throughout the series, she creates anticipation that pulls readers through the middle books.

Your story idea needs to support expansion, too. This is where understanding your natural storytelling ecosystem becomes crucial. Take Terry Pratchett's *Discworld* series. Forty-one books set in the same world, yet they never feel repetitive. Why? Because Pratchett built a world flexible enough to support multiple story types. He could write police procedurals, political satires, coming-of-age stories, and philosophical explorations all within the same framework. The world became a platform for exploring different ideas rather than a constraint.

This kind of flexibility requires careful foundation building. When you're developing your initial story idea, ask yourself:

Does this world have enough complexity to support multiple stories? Not just in terms of plot, but in terms of themes, conflicts, and character types.

What different angles could you explore? A good story world offers multiple entry points and perspectives. The *Star Wars* universe supports everything from epic space opera to intimate character studies like *The Mandalorian*.

Where are the natural tension points? Sustainable stories often have built-in conflicts that generate plots naturally. The class divisions in *The Hunger Games* create endless opportunities for story development.

But sustainability isn't just about building big. Sometimes it means knowing when to reset and scale back. *The Vampire Diaries* hit this point when their stakes kept escalating until they literally couldn't go higher. They had to deliberately reset to more personal, grounded stories to keep the series viable. This kind of strategic scaling requires understanding both your story's limits and your audience's needs.

This applies even if you're writing standalone novels. Every story needs enough depth to sustain reader interest through multiple acts. By thinking in terms of story sustainability from the start, you build richer worlds and more engaging narratives, regardless of your ultimate story length.

SEASONAL PATTERNS AND MARKET POSITIONING

Most writing advice focuses on craft and structure, but timing can make or break your story's success. We're not just talking about the obvious seasonal connections, either. Obviously, horror selling better in October or romance spiking around Valentine's Day are easily recognizable trends, but understanding deeper patterns in reader psychology and cultural cycles helps you position your stories for maximum impact.

For instance, did you know that dystopian fiction typically sells better when times are good? During periods of actual social upheaval, readers often gravitate toward more optimistic stories. This seems backward until you consider reader psychology. When life feels stable, people can safely explore darker themes. When reality itself feels dystopian, readers often seek escape and hope.

Squid Games demonstrates perfect cultural timing. The show captured something specific about our collective experience during the pandemic - the feeling of being trapped, competing for survival while trying to maintain humanity. That same show released five years earlier or later might not have resonated nearly as powerfully. Context matters.

Summer reading patterns differ significantly from winter ones, and not just in obvious ways. During summer months, readers often tackle heavier content, particularly in romance and thriller genres. This isn't random. It reflects deeper psychological patterns. When people feel generally more positive (hello, sunshine), they're better equipped emotionally to handle challenging content. Winter drives readers toward comfort reads like cozy mysteries and sweet romances that provide emotional warmth during cold months.

This isn't always true, of course, as people love a good beach read in the summer, but you might find your dark, brooding book too much for people while they are already in the winter doldrums.

Taylor Swift masters this kind of seasonal positioning. During the pandemic, she released two related albums in "Folklore" and "Evermore." Though created as sister albums, she positioned them differently. "Folklore" captured end-of-summer melancholy, while "Evermore" embraced winter themes and darker tones. Same creative period, different seasonal resonance.

Smart authors can apply this thinking to their own work. One fascinating example comes from Melanie Harlow, who skillfully repositions the same book for different seasons. A romance that emphasizes its Christmas elements during holiday promotions might focus on its small-town aspects during summer. The key isn't changing the story but highlighting different elements that naturally resonate at different times.

This requires building enough genuine depth into your concept to support multiple angles. A movie like *Die Hard* works as both an action movie and a Christmas film because those elements exist naturally within the story. The Christmas setting isn't just decoration, either. It adds emotional weight to John McClane's motivation to reconnect with his family. This kind of organic layering gives you more flexibility.

Cultural cycles affect genre popularity too. Romance thrives during economic downturns because people crave guaranteed happy endings. Fantasy often surges during periods of social change as readers seek metaphorical ways to process real-world transitions. Understanding these patterns helps you position your work effectively.

The key is to match your story's natural strengths to appropriate seasonal and cultural moments. A dark thriller might fare better in summer than winter. A cozy mystery series might plan holiday-themed releases to capitalize on seasonal reader preferences. But these choices should grow organically from your story rather than feeling forced.

Consider how different story elements resonate seasonally:

- Food scenes hit differently during holiday seasons
- Outdoor adventures connect more strongly during summer
- Family dynamics resonate particularly during holiday periods
- Personal transformation stories spike around New Year
- Academic settings naturally align with school year timing

Building awareness of these patterns into your story development gives you more flexibility in positioning your work. You're not changing your story to fit the market - you're identifying natural connections between your story elements and reader rhythms.

BUILDING BETTER STORY IDEAS

We've covered a lot of ground about what makes ideas work but now let's dig into the how. After years of studying successful stories and working with authors, we've developed specific techniques for strengthening story ideas. None of these are magic formulas - they're tools you can use to enhance your natural creativity.

The first technique we call idea smashing, and it's exactly what it sounds like. Take your story concepts and crash them together like kids playing with toy cars. This isn't a random combination. It's about finding unexpected connections that create new possibilities.

Let's walk through an example. Say you want to write a romance, and you've got these elements floating around:

- A small-town coffee shop
- A character who can see ghosts
- A family curse
- A Christmas festival

The obvious approach might be to write either a sweet small-town romance or a paranormal romance. But what happens when you combine elements? Maybe your coffee shop owner discovers they can see ghosts after drinking a particular coffee blend. Maybe the family curse ties to the Christmas festival. Suddenly you've got something that could work as paranormal romance, cozy mystery, or even magical realism depending on which elements you emphasize.

One technique we see newer writers struggle with is what we call "trope stacking." They worry using familiar tropes will make their story feel derivative. But here's the truth - tropes are just building blocks. The art lies in how you combine and transform them. *Bridgerton* doesn't avoid romance tropes; it layers them skillfully with historical elements and modern sensibilities to create something that feels fresh.

When you're developing your idea, start collecting tropes that naturally fit your story. Then look for ways to twist or combine them. If you're writing enemies-to-lovers, what happens if you add a forced proximity situation? What if one character has a secret identity? Each additional layer creates new possibilities for conflict and connection.

This brings us to our next technique: identifying your story's natural expansions. Every strong idea has room to grow in multiple directions. Let's use *Legends and Lattes* as an example - a cozy fantasy about an orc opening a coffee shop. The initial concept might seem limited, but consider the natural expansion points:

- Other fantasy races discovering coffee
- Magical coffee blends
- Competition from established taverns
- Community relationships and regular customers
- Supply chain adventures for exotic ingredients

Each of these directions could support additional stories while maintaining the core appeal of the original concept.

Testing your concept's strength isn't about whether it sounds good in a pitch meeting. Ask yourself: *Does this idea generate a story naturally, or am I forcing conflict? Could this concept support multiple character arcs without feeling stretched? Does it offer various entry points for different types of readers? Are there natural ways to raise stakes without breaking the story's internal logic? Can this idea evolve without losing its core appeal?*

The goal isn't to create a perfectly engineered story that feels soulless. The goal is to enhance your natural creativity with structural understanding. These techniques aren't rules to follow but tools to use when needed.

Throughout this chapter, we've explored the anatomy of ideas that stick with readers. From that even the most brilliant concept is just a starting point. The real art lies in development - taking that initial spark and building it into something that captures readers' imagination while maintaining enough depth to reward their investment. By understanding these principles and applying them thoughtfully to your unique story, you can craft ideas that don't just hook readers but keep them coming back for more.

The best stories feel both surprising and inevitable. They shock us with their novelty while satisfying deep emotional needs we might not even have recognized. That's the kind of storytelling we're aiming for, and with these tools and insights, you're ready to start developing ideas that achieve exactly that.

PSYCHOLOGICAL TRIGGERS

Authors have always found compelling ways to engage readers through plot, character, and world building, but by consciously incorporating psychological triggers into storytelling, we can create even deeper resonance that makes stories truly unforgettable. You've likely encountered books that stayed with you long after reading, touching something fundamental in your experience of being human.

The challenge lies not just in crafting good sentences or plotting engaging storylines, but in weaving psychological elements that tap into readers' natural emotional responses. Rather than trying to force engagement through dramatic events or beautiful prose alone, psychological triggers work with readers' innate processing of storylines, making emotional connection feel natural and inevitable.

Consider how you become invested in a story. You don't continue reading just because the writing is polished, or the plot is clever. Instead, you go through a journey of discovery, forming emotional connections with characters and situations that mirror deep human experiences. This same principle applies to crafting scenes and character arcs that truly resonate.

The key difference between technically proficient writing and deeply affecting storytelling lies in the depth of psychological engagement. While basic craft focuses on clear narrative and compelling events, psychological triggers build emotional investment. They create a foundation of authentic human experience that makes readers not just intellectually engaged but viscerally connected to your story.

This approach requires understanding five crucial types of psychological triggers that influence how readers process storylines. Each trigger serves a specific purpose in building authentic narrative resonance, and when used together, they create a comprehensive framework for writing stories that stay with readers long after the last page.

BUILDING MEANINGFUL CONNECTIONS

At their heart, successful stories create deep connections through layers of meaning and emotional resonance. Just as a garden grows through careful cultivation rather than mechanical planting, stories flourish when each element is thoughtfully developed to engage readers on multiple levels. Your scenes and characters should invite readers to explore, discover, and connect with the deeper truths woven throughout your narrative.

When you move beyond surface-level storytelling to create psychological depth, readers transform from passive observers into engaged participants in the journey you've crafted. They become invested not just in plot outcomes, but in the thematic and emotional discoveries along the way. This is the difference between writing a story and creating an experience that stays with readers.

Consider how the most memorable stories work. They don't just present events. They create spaces for readers to explore meaning, discover connections, and engage with ideas that resonate with their own experiences. Each scene serves multiple purposes, operating on both plot and psychological levels simultaneously.

The magic happens when you view your story elements as opportunities for deeper engagement rather than just plot devices. Character choices, setting details, and even dialogue can tap into fundamental human experiences and emotions. When readers connect on this level, they naturally invest in the journey you're creating.

This approach requires understanding that every story element is an opportunity to deepen psychological engagement. Whether through character relationships, thematic exploration, or emotional revelations, each component should contribute to the reader's deeper experience of the story.

Think about the stories that have stayed with you longest. Is it just their plots you remember, or the way they made you feel part of something larger? This same principle applies to your writing. When you focus on creating meaningful psychological resonance, reader engagement naturally follows.

The key is authenticity in how you develop these psychological elements. Readers can sense when emotional moments feel forced versus organically developed. This authenticity, combined with deliberate use of psychological triggers, creates stories that feel both natural and profound.

We're about to explore specific psychological triggers that make this approach work but remember: the foundation of all memorable stories lies in genuine psychological resonance. Without this foundation, even the cleverest plots or beautiful prose will fail to truly move readers.

WHY DO WE NEED PSYCHOLOGICAL TRIGGERS?

Traditional writing often focuses on what we might call "surface engagement," which are those story elements that immediately grab readers through clear genre markers, familiar tropes, or compelling hooks. While these elements are important, they only reach readers already primed to connect with your type of story.

But focusing solely on these surface elements means missing opportunities to create deeper resonance. Even if someone enjoys fantasy novels, they might not fully engage with your fantasy story without deeper psychological anchoring. The key lies in weaving multiple layers of psychological connection throughout your narrative.

This is where psychological triggers become crucial. Instead of relying on plot or genre conventions alone, we use five powerful elements to create multiple pathways for reader engagement:

- Core Wounds
- Pleasure and Pain Inducers
- X-Factors
- Connection Deepeners
- Button-Pushers

Each trigger addresses different aspects of how readers connect with the story, allowing your narrative to resonate on multiple psychological levels simultaneously.

The more psychological layers you build into your story, the more opportunities you create for meaningful connection. One reader might connect with your character's internal struggles (Core Wounds), while another responds to the thematic exploration of fundamental fears. Someone else might be drawn in by the unique perspective you bring (X-Factor), while others engage with the transformational journey you've crafted.

By moving beyond surface engagement, you're not just writing a story - you're creating an experience that resonates on multiple psychological levels. This approach requires more careful crafting, but it results in something far more valuable: stories that stay with readers long after they finish the last page.

These psychological elements work together to create stories that don't just entertain but leave lasting impressions that change how readers see themselves and their world.

UNDERSTANDING CORE WOUNDS

When we talk about core wounds in writing, we're exploring something far deeper than simple pain points or customer needs. These are the fundamental emotional injuries that shape how people view themselves and interact with the world. Think of them as the deep grooves in our psychological landscape, carved by experiences often dating back to childhood.

Core wounds manifest in six primary transformational paths, each representing a journey from pain to healing:

- **Rejection to Acceptance:** This wound centers on the deep human need to belong. People carrying this wound constantly seek validation, afraid they'll never truly fit in. Your writing might speak to how your work helps readers find their tribe or validates their experiences.
- **Control to Surrender:** Here we find people struggling with uncertainty and chaos. They grip tightly to whatever they can control, often missing the beauty of letting go. Your content could explore how embracing uncertainty leads to unexpected gifts.
- **Abandonment to Integration:** This wound touches on our fear of being left behind or forgotten. Those carrying this wound often struggle to trust or form deep connections. Your messaging might focus on building lasting relationships and creating stable foundations.
- **Shame to Honor:** Perhaps one of the most profound wounds, shame makes people feel inherently flawed or unworthy. Your writing could demonstrate pathways to self-acceptance and pride in one's authentic self.
- **Betrayal to Devotion:** This wound impacts how people trust and form relationships. Those carrying it often expect to be let down or deceived. Your content might explore themes of loyalty, trust-building, and genuine connection.
- **Injustice to Equality:** This wound stems from experiences of unfairness or discrimination.

> People carrying it are highly attuned to power imbalances and seek level playing fields.

The power of understanding these core wounds lies in how we use them. It's not about exploiting pain points, creating genuine paths to healing. When you structure your story around addressing these wounds, you're not just writing a book; you're offering a transformation both to your character and your reader.

If you're writing a fantasy novel about an outcast who finds their place in the world, you're speaking directly to the rejection-to-acceptance wound. The key is authenticity. *Readers can sense when you're genuinely addressing their deep emotional needs versus simply using their pain to make a sale.* This is why the most effective books often come from authors who have worked through these same wounds themselves. They can speak to both the pain and the possibility of healing from a place of genuine understanding.

What makes core wounds such a powerful foundation for writing is their universality. While we might experience them differently, these fundamental hurts are part of the human experience. By acknowledging and addressing them respectfully, we create books that resonate on a profound level, making readers feel truly seen and understood.

The goal isn't to fix these wounds. That's beyond the scope of what we do as writers. Instead, we're creating safe spaces where these wounds can be acknowledged, understood, and gently tended. This approach transforms writing into a healing journey that benefits both author and reader.

PLEASURE AND PAIN INDUCERS

At our core, humans experience the world through two fundamental lenses: pleasure and pain. These emotional experiences drive our decision-making in profound and often unconscious ways. Understanding how to work with these emotional drivers can transform your writing from mere promotion to meaningful engagement.

We might consider ourselves "logical creatures", but emotions drive decisions, and logic justifies them after the fact. You can come up with rational reasons to justify any decision, but the initial impulse was purely emotional. This is how the human brain works. *Emotion leads and logic follows.*

In writing, pleasure and pain inducers serve as emotional resonance points. They help readers connect with your work on a visceral level. A romance novel doesn't just tell a love story. It taps into the pleasure of falling in love and the pain of loneliness. A thriller doesn't just offer suspense. It plays with the pleasure of solving mysteries and the pain of uncertainty.

The key is understanding that these emotional triggers aren't meant to manipulate. Instead, they're meant to create authentic connections. *When you share your own experiences with pleasure and pain in your writing, you're inviting readers into a shared emotional space.* You're saying, "I understand what you're feeling because I've felt it too."

Consider how this works in practice. Let's say you're writing a self-help book about personal growth. Instead of just focusing on its features ("10 chapters of actionable advice!"), you might tap into:

The pain points:

- The frustration of feeling stuck
- The exhaustion of trying and failing
- The fear of never reaching your potential

And balance them with pleasure points:

- The joy of breakthrough moments
- The satisfaction of personal progress
- The excitement of discovering new possibilities

It's a balance, and they work best in parity with each other. You can't focus too heavily on pain points by creating writing that feels heavy and depressing, nor can you lean too far into pleasure, making promises that feel unrealistic. The magic lies in acknowledging the pain while illuminating the path to pleasure.

Your writing should create an emotional arc. Start by showing readers you understand their current emotional state (*often pain-based*). Then, guide them through the possibility of transformation, painting a vivid picture of what could be (*pleasure-based*). Finally, position your work as the bridge between these two states.

This approach works because it mirrors how we naturally process emotional experiences. Most of the time, we don't jump directly from pain to pleasure. We need to feel understood in our current state before we're ready to envision change. Your writing should honor this journey, creating space for both the current reality and the potential future.

One powerful technique is to develop emotional echoes. These are recurring themes or phrases that resonate with both the pain and pleasure aspects of your readers' experiences. For example, "From overwhelmed to overjoyed" or "Transform your struggle into strength." These paired concepts create emotional bookends that readers can relate to.

It's important to note here that readers in some genres (*like romcom*) want very little pain and a lot of pleasure while readers of others (*like grimdark*) are there, at least partially, for the pain.

Remember, *every reader is on their own emotional journey*. Your job isn't to force them into feeling certain emotions, but to create writing that recognizes and respects where they are while gently illuminating where they could be. This approach builds trust and creates deeper connections than traditional feature-focused writing ever could.

By unlocking more pain and pleasure inducers in your writing, you can give permission for more people to read your work. Maybe one pain inducer is clear from your cover and blurb, but if you embed several more into your work, and unearth them through your writing, you can exponentially increase your market.

X-FACTOR

In today's market, being good at writing is not enough anymore. The market is flooded with talented authors, all vying for readers' attentions. This is where the X-Factor comes into play. It positions you several steps ahead of your audience and establishes you as someone worth following, not just another voice in the crowd.

Think of the X-Factor as your unique value proposition, but with a crucial twist. *It's not just about what makes you different, but what makes you a natural leader for your specific audience.* When you properly establish your X-Factor, readers don't just buy your books. They join your movement.

Consider Brandon Sanderson. He's not just writing fantasy novels, but an entire universe of intricate magic all while hosting a community filled with hundreds of thousands of loyal readers. His X-Factor isn't just his writing ability but lies in his ability to make readers feel like they're part of the creative journey.

The X-Factor works by providing two critical elements: heroes to look up to and "aha moments" that transform readers' lives. These aha moments are particularly powerful because they create lasting connections.

When a reader experiences an insight or breakthrough because of your work, they're much more likely to become a loyal follower.

Your X-Factor isn't just about your credentials or achievements. It's about how you use your experience and expertise to inspire action in others. *If you've overcome significant obstacles to write your books, that journey becomes part of your X-Factor.* If you have unique professional experience that informs your writing, that's part of your X-Factor too.

The most effective way to establish your X-Factor is through what I call "leadership positioning." *This means consistently demonstrating not just what you know, but how that knowledge or experience benefits your readers.* It's about creating a clear path between your expertise and your readers' desired outcomes.

One of the hardest truths for authors to process is that none of this, not one word that you've ever written, no matter how personal, is about you. It's all about your reader using your work as a conduit to explore their own transformation.

Your X-Factor should make it clear why you're the right person to guide readers through this transformation. This might mean sharing behind-the-scenes glimpses of your creative process, explaining how your life experiences inform your writing, or demonstrating your deep understanding of the genres or topics you write about.

Importantly, your X-Factor should inspire readers to listen and take action. If you're writing historical fiction, your X-Factor might be your unique approach to research that brings forgotten stories to life. If you're writing self-help, it might be your proven method for achieving specific results. Whatever it is, it should give readers a compelling reason to choose your work over others in your field.

The beauty of developing a strong X-Factor is that it makes marketing feel more natural. Instead of awkwardly promoting your books, you're sharing valuable insights and experiences that naturally lead readers to want more of what you offer. It transforms marketing from pushing sales to pulling readers into your world.

CONNECTION DEEPENERS

Think of Connection Deepeners as bridges between you and your readers, just not the mass-produced steel and concrete kind. These are more like handcrafted wooden bridges, each one unique, built with care and attention to the specific landscape they span.

The fascinating thing about Connection Deepeners is that they work by creating resonance with your audience in ways that go beyond just your books. When used effectively, they help readers feel truly seen and understood, often in ways they didn't realize they needed.

Meeting readers where they are is crucial to this process. This means understanding that every reader comes to your work with their own context, their own struggles, their own hopes. Instead of expecting readers to adapt to your world, you're creating points of connection that feel natural and intuitive to them.

What makes Connection Deepeners particularly powerful is that they give readers a shared language to communicate with each other. *When you create terms, phrases, or concepts that resonate with your audience, you're not just building individual connections, you're fostering a community.* Consider how Terry Pratchett fans immediately understand references to "The Luggage" or how Stephen King readers share a special understanding of "The Dark Tower." These aren't just story elements, but community touchstones.

What's often overlooked is how Connection Deepeners work beyond the obvious fan-author relationship. *They create reader-to-reader bonds that strengthen your entire community.* This is why successful authors often find their readers forming book clubs, fan groups, or online communities without direct author involvement. The connections you create become self-sustaining.

The most powerful aspect of Connection Deepeners is their ability to make readers feel like their truest selves in your community. This isn't about creating a false sense of belonging - it's about providing safe spaces where readers can explore, express, and embrace who they really are. When readers feel this level of acceptance and understanding, they become more than just consumers of your work - they become active participants in your author journey.

Remember that scene in "Dead Poets Society" where students stand on their desks to see the world differently? *That's what Connection Deepeners do.* They offer new perspectives, new ways of seeing and understanding, that readers carry with them long after they've finished your books.

BUTTON-PUSHERS

Button-Pushers are those subtle yet powerful elements that transform interest into action. They're what makes someone stop scrolling, click through, and ultimately make a purchase. But they're not just about driving sales; they're about creating those magical moments where a reader thinks, "Yes, this is exactly what I've been looking for."

I call this process of realization the "snap, snap, snap." Picture what happens at a successful book signing. There's that moment when someone sees your book and something catches their eye. That's the first "snap," or *the stop*. Then, they read the back cover or a random passage that speaks directly to them. That's the second "snap," or *the click*. Finally, they walk to the register, book in hand. That's the third "snap," or *the buy*. These three snaps aren't random. They're carefully orchestrated moments of connection.

What makes Button-Pushers so powerful is their ability to work at a subconscious level. *When you use them effectively, readers don't feel pushed or manipulated. They feel drawn in, compelled by their own curiosity and desire.* It's like creating a path of breadcrumbs that leads readers naturally to the next step.

Button-Pushers aren't about being clever or manipulative. They're about being so genuinely compelling that readers can't help but want to engage further. When you share a story that resonates deeply with your audience, when you tap into their genuine desires and aspirations, you're not pushing buttons - you're opening doors.

The real magic happens when Button-Pushers align with genuine value. Your goal isn't just to get someone to buy your book; it's to ensure they're genuinely excited to read it. Think about how Netflix gets you to watch "just one more episode" - not through force, but by understanding and delivering exactly what you want next.

Used effectively, Button-Pushers help potential readers self-identify. They think, "This author gets me" or "This is exactly what I need right now." When this happens, you've created something powerful - a connection that goes beyond the transaction to create genuine anticipation and excitement.

Remember, the ultimate goal isn't just to make the sale - it's to create such a compelling case for your work that readers can't wait to dive in.

UNDERSTANDING LIFE'S TRANSITIONS

Above psychological triggers, one other powerful thing to consider with your writing is focusing on specific *transition points.* Every significant change in life creates a moment of psychological openness, a time when people are more receptive to new ideas, solutions, and perspectives.

Think of transitions like a house during renovation. When the walls are stripped bare and the floors are being replaced, that's when you can make the biggest changes. Similarly, when people are going through major life transitions, their normal patterns and resistances are disrupted, creating unique opportunities for meaningful connection.

What makes transitions such powerful moments to focus? During times of change, people experience what psychologists call "identity plasticity" when their sense of self becomes more flexible and open to transformation. This isn't just about being more likely to buy. It's about being more receptive to deep, meaningful engagement with content that speaks to their current experience.

Consider the common transitions we all face: graduating from school, starting a new job, entering or leaving relationships, becoming parents, changing careers, moving cities, facing health challenges, or retiring. Each of these moments creates a psychological state where people actively seek guidance, understanding, and support. They're not just looking for solutions; they're looking for meaning and connection during times of uncertainty.

The key to leveraging transition points effectively lies in understanding their emotional architecture. Every transition contains three essential elements:

First, there's *the letting go phase,* where people release old patterns, identities, or situations. This often involves grief, uncertainty, and anxiety, even when the change is positive.

Your writing can acknowledge and validate these complex emotions.

Second comes the *neutral zone*, the uncomfortable period between the old and the new. This is where people feel most vulnerable but also most open to new perspectives. Your content can provide guidance and reassurance during this crucial phase.

Finally, there's *the new beginning* where people establish fresh patterns and identities. This is when they're actively seeking tools, communities, and frameworks to support their emerging reality.

What makes transitions particularly powerful is that people in transition are actively engaged in self-directed change. *They're not passive consumers waiting to be sold to, but active seekers looking for resources that speak to their experience.* This creates natural openings for authentic connection and meaningful engagement.

Your task as a marketer is to identify which transition points align naturally with your work. What moments of change does your content speak to? When are people most likely to need what you offer? Understanding these intersections allows you to create books that feel less like telling a story and more like extending a helping hand at exactly the right moment.

EXAMPLES THAT TIE IT ALL TOGETHER

Now that we have all the pieces, let's talk about transitions and their psychological triggers in a way that feels more concrete.

THE NEW PARENT

Think about someone who's just become a new parent. They're in a massive life transition - probably sleep-deprived, overwhelmed, and questioning everything. This is a perfect moment to connect with readers because during transitions, people actively seek solutions and support. They're hungry for guidance.

Their core wound might be feeling utterly unprepared or isolated. So, if you write parenting books, you don't just market your "how-to" guide. You speak to that deep feeling of uncertainty. You might share your own stumbling first weeks of parenthood (*Connection Deepener*), demonstrate your expertise through specific, relatable situations (*X-Factor*), and show the pleasure of moving from chaos to confidence.

Or consider someone going through a divorce. They're dealing with a profound sense of failure (*Core Wound*), questioning their identity, and facing an uncertain future. If you write self-discovery novels or personal growth books, this transition moment is rich with potential connection points. Your books might emphasize the journey from betrayal to trust, from brokenness to wholeness.

Career changes are another powerful transition point. Someone leaving corporate life to start their own business is experiencing multiple psychological triggers simultaneously, like fear of failure, dreams of independence, and a need for validation. If you write business books or even fiction about personal reinvention, this transition provides natural connection points.

The key is recognizing that transitions create openings for deeper engagement because people in transition are actively looking for:

- Validation of their feelings
- Guidance through uncertainty
- Hope for the future
- Community of others in similar situations

CAREER BURNOUT

Let's explore another powerful transition moment: career burnout. This is fascinating because it combines both professional and deeply personal psychological triggers.

Picture someone in their mid-thirties who's achieved everything they thought they wanted. They have a good job, decent salary, and respectable title. But they're exhausted, unfulfilled, and quietly wondering "Is this all there is?" This transition point is particularly rich because it involves multiple core wounds: the shame of feeling ungrateful for a "good" job, the fear of starting over, and often a deep sense of betrayal (*either by the system or their own choices*).

If you write inspirational fiction or career transformation books, this transition creates natural connection points. The core wound here isn't just about career frustration - it's about identity. Who are you when the career you've built stops defining you? This is where pleasure and pain inducers become incredibly powerful.

The pain points are vivid: Sunday night anxiety, feeling trapped in golden handcuffs, watching life pass by in endless Zoom meetings. But the pleasure points are equally compelling: rediscovering passion, feeling alive again, building something meaningful. Your writing might weave these together, showing understanding of both the current pain and the potential for transformation.

Your X-Factor might come from having made this journey yourself, or from guiding others through it. You're not just offering escape; you're providing a roadmap through the wilderness of career reinvention. This resonates particularly strongly because people in career transitions are often looking for both practical guidance and emotional support.

The Connection Deepeners here could focus on shared experiences that often go unspoken - the guilt of wanting more, the fear of disappointing family, the secret relief of finally admitting you need change. When you name these experiences, readers feel seen and understood, often for the first time.

Button-Pushers in this context might focus on the cost of staying stuck versus the potential of change. Not in a manipulative way, but by reflecting real questions your readers are already asking themselves: "What's the real price of another year in this job?" "What possibilities am I never giving myself permission to explore?"

This transition point is especially powerful because it often coincides with other life transitions - relationships, health, personal identity. It's a moment when people are particularly receptive to new ideas and perspectives, making them more likely to engage deeply with content that speaks to their experience.

During career burnout transitions, people are actively seeking:

- Validation that their dissatisfaction is legitimate and significant, not just ingratitude or weakness
- Evidence that change is possible - not just inspirational stories, but concrete paths forward
- Permission to prioritize fulfillment over traditional metrics of success
- Frameworks to help them imagine and build a different future

MOVING TO A NEW CITY

Let's explore the transition of moving to a new city - a moment that combines external change with profound internal shifts.

Picture someone who's just accepted a job in a new city. On the surface, it's about logistics, like finding an apartment, learning new routes, and setting up utilities. But underneath, this person is wrestling with deeper questions about identity, community, and belonging. They're literally and figuratively mapping out a new life.

This transition is particularly rich because it often involves mourning what's left behind while simultaneously building something new. The core wound here centers on belonging - the fear of being perpetually "new," of losing established connections, of having to rebuild from scratch in an unfamiliar environment.

If you write contemporary fiction, self-help, or even city-specific guides, this transition creates powerful connection opportunities. You're catching readers at a moment when their normal support systems are disrupted and they're actively seeking new connections and guidance. The pleasure and pain points here are deeply intertwined - the excitement of new possibilities exists alongside the anxiety of unknown challenges.

Your X-Factor might be having made multiple successful moves yourself, understanding the emotional landscape of relocation, or having deep knowledge of building community in new places. You're not just offering practical advice; you're providing emotional scaffolding for this major life change.

During relocation transitions, people are actively seeking:

- Reassurance that their mix of excitement and grief is normal and valid
- Practical tools for building social connections from scratch
- Guidance on maintaining old relationships while creating new ones
- Ways to preserve their identity while adapting to a new environment

TRANSFORMING YOUR BOOK INTO A GRIPPING READ

As we've explored the intricate landscape of psychological triggers, one fundamental truth emerges: successful books are not about selling, but about connecting. It's about creating a bridge between your work and the readers who need it most, understanding that every book is more than just a product. It's a potential transformation waiting to happen.

The strategies we've discussed—*Core Wounds, Pleasure and Pain Inducers, X-Factor, Connection Deepeners*, and

Button-Pushers—are not manipulative tactics, but genuine pathways to meaningful engagement. They represent a profound shift from traditional approaches that treat readers as passive consumers to a more holistic model that sees readers as active participants in a shared journey.

Remember, your book is a vehicle for connection, not just information or entertainment. Every reader comes to your work with their own story, their own struggles, and their own hopes. Your books should honor that complexity, creating spaces where readers feel truly seen and understood.

The most powerful writing happens when you are trying to serve. This means:

- Deeply understanding the transitions and challenges your readers face
- Sharing your authentic journey with vulnerability and courage
- Creating content that goes beyond your books to address fundamental human experiences
- Building communities that support and uplift readers

Ultimately, successful writing is about trust. Trust that develops not through aggressive promotion, but through consistent, genuine connection. It's about showing readers that you understand them, that you're committed to their growth and transformation, and that your work is a tool for their own personal journey.

Your words have power, not just on the page, but in the lives of those who read them. Writing, when done with empathy and insight, becomes an extension of that power. It's an invitation, a bridge, a helping hand extended to readers who are seeking something more than just another book.

So, step forward with confidence. Your writing is not about shouting into the void, but about creating meaningful dialogue. It's about turning the solitary act of writing into a collaborative experience of human connection. In a world hungry for authenticity, your genuine approach will not just sell books. It will create a lasting impact.

UNIVERSAL FANTASIES AND TROPES

There's a particular moment, sometime after you've nailed down your plot and cast of characters, when you realize how urgently you want your story to spark that visceral "I have to keep reading" response. It's tempting to believe this spark comes from a shiny concept or a perfectly executed plot twist, but time and again, we see stories that seem straightforward or even quiet ignite massive fandoms and global followings. They usually do so, as Theodora Taylor observes in *7 Figure Fiction*, because they touch on what she calls universal fantasies, or deep-seated desires and dreams so fundamental that readers can't help but respond.

Taylor's premise, gleaned from years of both writing and marketing her own bestselling romances, is that these universal fantasies speak directly to our most human cravings. We want to feel safe, or chosen, or forgiven, or recognized as special. We want to believe in second chances and in the unconditional acceptance that says, "You are worthy no matter what."

When a book harnesses one or more of these yearnings, something almost magical happens: the story slips beneath the reader's guard and becomes personal. The desire might be coded differently, depending on the genre, but it's always there, silent and steady, like an underground river feeding every page.

In *7 Figure Fiction*, Taylor breaks down how these fantasies show up across genres. In romance, it's often the promise that real love can withstand any trial, even the ones we're convinced should scare people away. In thrillers, it might be the longing for competence, the idea that an ordinary person can rise to extraordinary circumstances and do something unbelievably heroic. In fantasy or sci-fi, it's the primal dream of power or the thrill of escapism: you're taken from your normal life and thrust into a realm that reveals your hidden strengths. Although these fantasies might wear different disguises, they share a root system: they nourish the belief that something vital—love, power, control, belonging, redemption—can triumph despite the worst odds.

Taylor's explanation resonates so strongly because she makes you see that these fantasies aren't a gimmick or marketing ploy; they are core to the human experience. If, for instance, your story shows someone who feels like an outsider finally finding a home, you're activating the universal fantasy of belonging. Readers who have ever felt alone, even briefly, will catch the emotional vibration. They might not articulate it as "I'm longing for a sense of home." They'll just *know* they can't stop reading because something about your character's journey mirrors a subtle but potent desire lurking inside them.

But how do these universal fantasies move from the abstract to the concrete details in your novel? One answer lies in *how* you choose to dramatize them. Imagine, for example, the universal fantasy of power, particularly the fantasy of being so competent that you can't be defeated. This is a staple of action thrillers and superhero tales: the unstoppable assassin with a heart of gold, or the woman with a haunted past who channels her trauma into a near-inhuman ability to protect herself and others. She might be battered and bruised, but her skill lifts her above the ordinary. She's not merely gifted. She's proof that self-mastery is possible in a chaotic world. It's a potent fantasy for anyone reading the story who's ever felt helpless.

The key is weaving that power fantasy into the familiar. If our assassin hero arrives fully formed on page one and never questions her competence or worthiness, readers might find her impressive but rarely intimate. A universal fantasy resonates best when it collides with vulnerability, like a core wound, an old regret, because then the fantasy becomes a narrative of triumph over adversity rather than a simplistic escapist thrill. We watch her wrestle with guilt over lives taken or relationships lost, and we see how her supernatural skill or cunning is both a blessing and a self-imposed prison. That emotional tension underscores the fantasy. Yes, we want to be that unstoppable, but not at the cost of our heart or our humanity.

UNIVERSAL STORY ENGINES

One of the points Theodora Taylor emphasizes in *7 Figure Fiction* is that universal fantasies, when harnessed well, are not merely decorative flairs. They become the driving energy of a story. A writer might outline a perfectly coherent plot, but if it doesn't press on a genuine human desire or dread, it risks feeling hollow. Conversely, a relatively simple plot can spark a massive response if the universal fantasy is front and center. Think about how many romance novels revolve around a small misunderstanding or an arranged marriage scenario, yet flourish because the longing to be chosen is so powerful.

In practice, your entire story architecture can revolve around how the protagonist seeks to fulfill the fantasy (or fears losing it). The external events, maybe an inheritance that requires marriage, a murder that your detective must solve, or a cosmic threat that upends your fantasy kingdom, are all vehicles for testing how badly your protagonist wants that emotional fulfillment. Are they someone who craves unconditional acceptance, so they hide their flaws lest people discover them? Do they yearn for redemption from a past mistake, so they take on dangerous missions hoping to balance invisible scales? Tying universal fantasies to the engine of your story ensures the emotional stakes stay high.

This is where we segue into another powerful framework: tropes. In many ways, tropes are the narrative skeletons that convey these fantasies to readers. Far from being cheap clichés, tropes often act like signposts that assure readers, "You'll get what you're longing for here, if you keep reading."

THE LANGUAGE OF TROPES

Jennifer Hilt's *Trope Thesaurus* has garnered attention among authors precisely because it recognizes that tropes are more than lazy formulas. They are, at heart, a vocabulary. Hilt argues that tropes form a sort of "book language" that readers learn over time. The moment a romance reader sees "secret baby," "enemies to lovers," or "forced proximity," they have a certain set of expectations. They might even have emotional triggers that activate. Someone who adores the "grumpy and sunshine" pairing, for instance, might get a spark of anticipation at the very mention of that dynamic.

Russell Nohelty

In the same way that people can watch a silent film and interpret the storyline through cinematic cues, readers understand tropes as coded signals. The presence of a "chosen one" in a fantasy novel tells them to expect a journey that challenges destiny versus free will, often coupled with a massive outpouring of heroic potential. They know they'll see that hero tested in ways that reflect the universal fantasy of fulfilling a grand purpose. That's not a "lazy device." It's akin to a shared language. If you, the writer, are aware of these signals and use them intentionally, you can drastically enhance a reader's immersion.

Hilt's perspective on tropes also allows you to see them as malleable. Rather than fixating on, "Oh, that's a cliché," you begin to think, "How can I transform or layer this trope in a fresh way?" Perhaps you keep the broad strokes but invert the power dynamic so that the familial feud is orchestrated by an outside force, and the lovers themselves are the only ones aware of the manipulation. That twist might preserve the core fantasy (love prevailing against impossible odds) while giving readers the sense that they're reading something both familiar and surprising.

While one trope is good, the real power comes from "stacking" tropes. She points out that many of the most successful novels pile on multiple tropes like a tapestry, so that different emotional promises are made simultaneously. A single fantasy romance novel could feature "friends to lovers" plus "snowed in together" plus "royalty in disguise" plus "amnesia." If this is done thoughtfully, each trope draws out a different emotional response. "Friends to lovers" hits the longing to be truly understood. The "snowed in" scenario intensifies forced proximity. The "royalty in disguise" toggles the fantasy of hidden power or glamour. "Amnesia" evokes the fear of lost identity, something that can heighten vulnerability. Together, these tropes form an intricately layered emotional experience, all pointing back to certain universal fantasies, safety, unconditional love, acceptance despite secrets, and so on.

What's fascinating is how Hilt echoes Theodora Taylor's argument in her own way. If universal fantasies are the deep wells of longing, tropes are the cups we use to scoop that water and deliver it to readers. One is the bedrock desire; the other is the recognized structure that effectively channels it.

READER CONTRACT

Reading any novel that uses a known trope is a bit like entering a contract. The writer promises an emotional outcome, and the reader consents to experience it. "Enemies to lovers" doesn't guarantee every beat, but it does provide a trajectory from mutual resentment to reluctant interest to unstoppable attraction. That's precisely why so many romance readers actively seek it out. The emotional tension inherent in that promise of "How will they go from hating each other to loving each other?" is addictive.

This contract can fall apart if you break the trope's fundamental appeal. If "enemies to lovers" is introduced, but the author rushes the transition in two pages with no real conflict resolution, the reader feels betrayed. The universal fantasy that someone who once saw the absolute worst in you might recognize your best is short-circuited. The tension dissolves unceremoniously, and the fantasy remains unfulfilled. Readers often describe such experiences as being "cheated," even if they can't articulate precisely why. They came for a certain emotional journey and got a half-baked product.

In that sense, tropes serve not only to entice readers but to keep you honest. They remind you of the emotional arc you're expected to deliver. If you're writing a thriller with the "lone wolf cop who breaks all the rules," you'd better show the cost of that approach, whether it's moral compromise, betrayal by trusted colleagues, or near-catastrophic misjudgment. Otherwise, the universal fantasy of unstoppable competence set against institutional red tape doesn't ring true. The moment you skip the emotional or logical steps, you violate the unspoken contract with your audience, and the tension dissipates.

FINDING YOUR WAY WITH TROPES

Writers sometimes worry about tropes "overshadowing" the unique aspects of their story. The real question is how to harness the comfort of the familiar while showcasing the distinct voice or twist that only *you* can bring. Take a classic trope like the "secret billionaire" in romance. The universal fantasy revolves around the idea that someone seemingly ordinary or even modest in circumstances is actually free from everyday burdens. They have the power to protect, provide, or pamper. Yet you can pivot from cliché into something personal by tying that wealth to a deeper wound, like perhaps the billionaire is haunted by the knowledge that their fortune came from unethical sources, and they've spent years trying to atone. Now, their love interest sees them not as a golden savior but as a partner wrestling with guilt and responsibility. The fantasy remains (a powerful protector) while the fresh nuance emerges (money as moral conflict).

Similarly, if you're weaving "found family" into a cozy mystery series, you can let that trope speak to the fantasy of unwavering belonging: no matter how eccentric or flawed you are, this ragtag group *wants* you around. But the "twist" might be that your amateur sleuth is actually hiding a connection to the crime, like maybe an unspoken past that links them to the victim's secrets. The "found family" trope becomes a catalyst for deeper emotional tension: will the sleuth's new support system accept them if the truth emerges? Now, the universal fantasies of belonging and safety are tested by fear of rejection, elevating a comfortable trope into something more suspenseful and personal.

What matters is that you allow the trope to do its job while you inject enough complexity to make the story distinct. You're not diminishing the trope's power; you're combining it with your unique voice, thematic concerns, or character arcs. In doing so, you create a reading experience that feels both comforting and surprising, two qualities that seldom coexist unless the author knows precisely which emotional levers they're pulling.

INTEGRATING TROPES AND UNIVERSAL FANTASIES

If universal fantasies are the intangible, often subconscious desires that drive readers, and tropes are the recognizable patterns that help fulfill these desires, there's a subtle interplay between the two that shapes every scene. It might look like this behind the scenes of your writing process:

1. **Identify the Core Wound**: Suppose your main character craves acceptance. Maybe because they've always been dismissed or ridiculed in their community.

2. **Choose a Trope That Amplifies That Longing**: You decide to put them in a "rivals to friends" situation at a new workplace, or a "boardroom battle" romance scenario where they clash with a boss or colleague, each trying to prove themselves. That trope becomes the structural framework for the acceptance vs. rejection tension.

3. **Layer Emotional Stakes**: The character's longing for acceptance isn't just a backstory detail. It influences their every interaction: how they approach group projects, how they react to the rival's criticism, how they either double down on their insecurities or lash out. The trope thrives on this tension.

4. **Deliver the Emotional Payoff**: Through crises, forced collaborations, or glimpses of vulnerability, the "rivals" slowly see each other's true worth. By the time they become more than friends, the universal fantasy and core wound of acceptance is realized. You haven't just told a "rivals to lovers" story, but you've also validated a deeper human need that resonates beyond the page.

Readers might not consciously name "universal fantasy of acceptance" as they read. They'll likely describe it as, "I loved how these two finally understood each other," or "It was so satisfying to see them both drop their walls." But what they're experiencing is the final wave of emotional relief that comes from seeing the longing answered. The trope of "rivals to lovers" was your vehicle, but the universal fantasy was your fuel.

Many authors find that repeatedly exploring a particular universal fantasy across multiple novels becomes a defining feature of their brand. Theodora Taylor, for example, has built a consistent readership by delivering certain emotional payoffs, like the "love that defies social expectation" or the "outsider who finds their perfect match." Jennifer Hilt's breakdown of tropes, meanwhile, encourages authors to see which patterns they gravitate toward. Maybe you always seem to write about hidden identities or second chances. That recurring pattern signals to readers the brand of emotional journey they can expect from you, no matter the specific storyline.

Over time, your mastery of certain tropes and universal fantasies can become a signature. Think about authors who are known for writing strong, tormented alpha heroes in romance. Their audience picks up each new release because they trust the author to deliver that specific emotional pitch: a man who's ferociously competent yet heartbreakingly wounded, and a woman who sees the hidden vulnerability beneath his gruff exterior. If this resonates with your brand, lean into it. If it doesn't, you might discover a different universal fantasy that forms the backbone of your storytelling identity.

Both Taylor and Hilt, in their respective works, unify under the idea that tropes are not constraints but a mutual language. If you picture the reading experience as a conversation between author and reader, tropes are the recognizable words and phrases that let readers know, "Ah, I understand what kind of story this is, and I'm here for it."

Meanwhile, universal fantasies are the emotional resonance that echoes in the background, coloring every word with personal significance.

The real craft lies in how you blend them. Too many tropes, and it can feel like an overstuffed, directionless story, an attempt to "please all fantasies" at once without giving each its proper focus. Too few universal fantasies, or ignoring them outright, and you risk writing a novel that might be academically clever but emotionally hollow. The middle path is about making sure that for every trope you introduce, you have at least one deep emotional current powering it. That way, your story is neither a meandering mash-up nor a dry conceptual exercise, but a living tapestry of emotional and narrative arcs.

Readers might then describe the experience in a starry-eyed review: "I fell in love with these characters and felt everything they went through." That's the moment you know you've successfully tapped into a universal fantasy and framed it with tropes that served as windows—clear enough for readers to see themselves but also tinted with your personal voice and creative vision.

CREATING AN UNBREAKABLE BOND

Ultimately, the reason universal fantasies and tropes work so well together is that they establish trust. Readers trust that if you use a particular trope, you know how to deliver the emotional beats they crave. They trust that the universal fantasy underpinning your novel will be honored. If you're promising an "ugly duckling turned shining star" arc, they expect that duckling to fight through adversity and find acceptance. If you promise the ultimate redemption arc for a villain-turned-hero, they anticipate a thorough exploration of regret, self-forgiveness, and transformation. These underlying assumptions form an unspoken pact. Break it, and you lose the bond with your audience. Fulfill it with skill and heart, and you gain not just readers, but advocates who recommend your books to everyone they know.

So, it's not just about sprinkling the right tropes or naming universal fantasies in your outline. It's about letting these fundamental desires shape every pivotal scene, every character decision, every emotional high and low. It's about remembering that you are, in many ways, writing for the secret hearts of your audience that yearns for that rescue, that redemption, and/or that triumphant unveiling. And it's about respecting the structures (tropes) that help convey that message, as well as the raw, human hunger (universal fantasies) that propels it.

When you strike this balance, you'll find that your story gains a certain gravitational pull. You can feel it when you reread a draft and realize you've woven in the perfect moment of revelation for a hero who desperately wants to be enough. You can see it in the ways your trope usage orchestrates the emotional confrontation your characters needed. You'll recognize it in the growing excitement of your beta readers, or in the flood of enthusiastic messages you start receiving from fans who say things like, "Your book felt like it was written just for me."

That's the sweet spot where universal fantasies meet the language of tropes. You've found a way to articulate both the silent longings of your audience and the structural promises that keep them turning pages. You've found your groove, your brand, and maybe even your writing destiny. And if you keep at it, layering in new angles, exploring different fantasies, flipping tropes on their heads without losing what made them powerful in the first place, then you'll discover that this approach isn't a trick or a hack. It's the very heart of why storytelling has captured human beings for millennia: we want to be seen, to be understood, to escape, to be free, to be chosen. And when you deliver that through stories, you become not just a writer, but a companion on the reader's own journey.

These strategies gift you the ability to craft tales so intimately aligned with what readers desire that they *must* keep reading, and by extension, must keep buying. It's a pragmatic approach to writing success, yes, but it's also deeply human. Because on the other side of every Amazon purchase, or every library checkout, stands a person who wants to believe in something bigger or truer or more beautiful about life. Whether that's redemption, revenge, love, or cosmic destiny, it's your job as the author to weave that fantasy in ways they can't resist.

In that sense, tropes and universal fantasies operate like an elegantly choreographed dance. One leads, the other follows, and they switch places sometimes, but together they spin out the story that will lodge in your reader's mind. The synergy is so seamless that readers might not even notice it consciously, yet the effect is undeniable. They close the book at three in the morning and stare at the ceiling, heart pounding with the echo of acceptance, or love, or unstoppable determination. And they say to themselves, "I can't wait to read whatever this author writes next."

When that happens, you've not only won a sale or a positive review. You've tapped into the hidden reservoir of primal wants that Theodora Taylor so wisely pinpoints, and you've used the elegantly coded language that Jennifer Hilt's troves of tropes provide. You've embraced your readers' yearnings at the deepest level and offered them a hopeful reflection of what they most want to see about themselves or the world. And that, in the grand tradition of storytelling, is the magic that transforms a mere collection of words on a page into an unforgettable, resonant experience.

Russell Nohelty

WRITING IN YOUR AUTHOR ECOSYSTEM

Writing has always been a deeply personal journey, yet for decades, authors have been squeezed into narrowly defined boxes of genre, style, and approach. Traditional publishing wisdom suggested a one-size-fits-all model of storytelling—learn the rules, follow the formula, and success will follow. But what if the key to unlocking your true writing potential lies not in conforming to external expectations, but in understanding your own unique Author Ecosystem?

The Author Ecosystems framework designed by Monica and I represents a revolutionary way of thinking about writing. Just as natural ecosystems in the world have distinct characteristics, each with its own balance, rhythm, and method of survival, so too do writers have inherent creative landscapes that shape how they approach storytelling.

Writers approach stories differently. While one writer might craft a narrative that precisely hits market trends, writing quickly and strategically, another would weave a deeply personal narrative, infusing the story with their unique perspective and creating a world that feels intimately connected to their own experiences. Neither approach is inherently superior. They are simply different expressions of creative energy.

That is the heart of the Author Ecosystems. It gives context to different ways to have success as an author.

This chapter explores how different Author Ecosystems manifest in both fiction and non-fiction writing. We'll journey through five distinct authorial landscapes: the trend-riding Desert, the depth-exploring Grassland, the excitement-generating Tundra, the personality-driven Forest, and the universe-building Aquatic. Each Ecosystem offers a unique lens through which stories are conceived, developed, and brought to life.

More than a writing guide, this exploration is an invitation to recognize and celebrate your natural creative tendencies. By understanding your Ecosystem, you can stop fighting against your inherent writing style and instead learn to harness its unique strengths.

THE DESERT

The first time Marco realized he was a Desert writer, he was staring at the *New York Times* bestseller list, a half-finished manuscript scattered across his desk. For years, he'd struggled to understand why his novels never quite caught fire. He'd pour his heart into intricate plotlines, only to watch them sink without a trace while seemingly formulaic books rocketed to success.

That morning, something clicked. It wasn't about writing the most beautiful book—it was about writing the right book at the right moment.

Russell Nohelty

Deserts are the literary world's most adaptable creatures. Like the resilient plants that thrive in arid landscapes, they don't fight the environment. They become masters of it. Their writing isn't about personal expression as much as it is about connection, about understanding the invisible currents of reader desire that flow beneath the surface of the literary marketplace.

Take romance novels, for instance. While some writers might spend months crafting a love story based purely on their personal vision, a Desert writer walks a more strategic path. They're not just telling a story. They're engaging in a sophisticated dialogue with readers' deepest current yearnings. When workplace romances start trending, they don't just notice. They understand why, and how to deliver a perfect experience for fans of that subgenre. Is it a reflection of changing professional dynamics? A desire for narratives of mutual respect? The Desert writer doesn't just observe these shifts; they translate them into narrative.

This doesn't make their work less creative. It requires the ability to be simultaneously responsive and original. It's like being a jazz musician who can improvise brilliantly within a specific musical framework, rather than a classical performer strictly following every note of the sheet music.

In non-fiction, this approach becomes even more pronounced. During the early months of the COVID-19 pandemic, Desert writers were the first to produce practical guides about remote work, mental health resilience, and navigating unprecedented personal challenges. They didn't wait for perfect information. They responded to an immediate need, providing clarity when readers were most hungry for understanding.

But this approach isn't without its challenges. The Desert ecosystem demands constant vigilance. It requires writers to be part storyteller, part cultural anthropologist who are always scanning, always listening. The risk is becoming so focused on trends that you lose the core of storytelling: genuine human connection.

The most successful Desert writers understand this delicate balance. They're not trend-chasers, but trend-interpreters. They don't just follow the market. They help shape it, offering narratives that feel simultaneously familiar and fresh.

For Marco, this realization was liberating. He stopped trying to write the book of his heart and started writing the book readers longed to read. His first trend-aligned novel didn't just sell, it resonated. Readers didn't just consume his story; they felt understood by it.

The Desert ecosystem isn't about sacrificing art for commerce. It's about recognizing that true art often lies in creating stories that speak directly to the moment, which help readers make sense of their rapidly changing world.

In the vast, shifting landscape of storytelling, Desert writers are the ultimate navigators. They don't fight the terrain. They become one with it.

THE GRASSLAND

Sarah's bookshelves told a story before she ever wrote a word. Each volume was meticulously researched, annotated, dog-eared. Where other writers collected books, she cultivated them like a careful gardener, understanding that true knowledge grows slowly, with patience and persistent care.

Grassland writers are the deep-root systems of the literary world. While other ecosystems might chase the quick bloom of trends or the flashy surface of storytelling, Grasslands are busy building entire worlds of understanding that can sustain readers for generations.

In fiction, this means creating universes so rich and comprehensive that readers don't just enter a story. They inhabit an entire ecosystem of imagination. George R.R. Martin didn't just write a fantasy series; he constructed a world so intricate that fans could spend decades exploring its history, linguistics, and cultural nuances. Each book becomes not just a narrative, but a gateway to a deeper, more complex understanding of human nature.

Non-fiction Grassland writers approach their subjects with similar depth. They aren't content with surface-level explanations or quick takes. When Yuval Noah Harari writes about human history, he's not simply recounting events. He's weaving a comprehensive understanding that connects seemingly disparate threads of human experience, showing how our past shapes our present and future.

This approach requires a kind of intellectual courage that goes beyond typical storytelling. Grassland writers must be willing to spend years developing a single concept. They understand that true expertise isn't about knowing everything quickly, but about knowing something so thoroughly that its complexity becomes beautiful.

Their writing process is less about productivity and more about exploration. Where a Desert writer might produce multiple books in a year, a Grassland writer might spend years on a single project, turning each idea like a gemstone, examining it from every possible angle. It's not inefficiency; it's commitment.

This doesn't mean Grassland writers are slow or academic. Their work pulses with life precisely because of its depth. They're not detached observers, but passionate investigators who bring entire worlds to life through meticulous research and profound insight.

In science fiction, this might mean creating technological systems so believable that they feel like blueprints for future innovation. In historical writing, it means reconstructing past worlds with such vivid detail that readers can smell the air, hear the conversations, understand the hidden motivations behind historical moments.

The greatest risk for a Grassland writer is getting lost in the details, becoming so fascinated by the complexity of their subject that they lose the narrative thread. The most successful Grasslands learn to balance depth with accessibility, creating work that is simultaneously scholarly and deeply engaging.

Sarah understood this. Her books weren't just stories or research. They were invitations asking readers to dig deeper, to see the world not as a collection of isolated facts, but as a complex, interconnected system waiting to be understood.

In a world that often celebrates speed and surface-level understanding, Grassland writers remind us that some stories require patience. Some truths can only be revealed through careful, persistent cultivation. They don't just write books. They grow entire worlds.

THE TUNDRA

The first time Kai realized he was a Tundra writer, he was standing at a convention, watching how a single book launch could transform an entire room's energy. It wasn't just about selling a book. It was about creating an event that people would remember.

Tundra writers are the performance artists of the literary world. Where other writers might see a book as a static object, Tundras see a living, breathing experience carefully orchestrated for maximum impact. Their writing isn't just about telling a story; it's about generating a wave of excitement that sweeps readers into an immersive narrative journey.

At the heart of the Tundra approach lies a masterful understanding of what makes stories compelling. These writers don't just use tropes. They stack them with surgical precision, creating narratives that hit multiple reader pleasure points simultaneously. Imagine a fantasy novel that combines the chosen one narrative, a complex magic system, and a found family arc. Each element is carefully selected not just for its individual appeal, but for how it interacts with the others, creating a narrative ecosystem more exciting than any single element could be.

This approach requires a deep, almost instinctual understanding of storytelling mechanics. Tundra writers are like literary DJs, mixing familiar beats in ways that feel both nostalgic and completely fresh. They know that readers don't want entirely new experiences. They want exciting reimaginings of stories they already love.

In non-fiction, this translates to books that feel like transformative events. A Tundra self-help author doesn't just offer advice. They create a narrative of personal revolution. They stack motivational techniques, personal anecdotes, and actionable strategies in a way that makes readers feel they're on the cusp of a life-changing moment.

The launch becomes as important as the book itself. Where other writers might see a book release as a simple transaction, Tundras see it as a carefully choreographed performance. They understand that excitement is a renewable resource. If managed correctly, each launch can feed into the next, creating a cycle of anticipation and satisfaction.

This doesn't mean their work is shallow. Far from it. The most successful Tundra writers understand that true excitement comes from depth carefully packaged in an accessible form. They're not afraid to tackle complex ideas, but they do so with a sense of narrative momentum that keeps readers turning pages.

Kai learned this lesson through years of trial and error. His early books were technically sound but lacked that spark of excitement. As he embraced his Tundra nature, he began to see each book as a carefully constructed experience. He didn't just write about a heist. He created a narrative that made readers feel like they were part of the most thrilling robbery in history.

The greatest challenge for Tundra writers is maintaining momentum. Their natural cycle is one of intense activity followed by periods of recovery. The most successful learn to use this rhythm, creating launches that feel like literary festivals, followed by thoughtful periods of reflection and preparation.

In a publishing world that often feels dominated by careful calculation or pure artistic expression, Tundra writers remind us that storytelling is also about joy, about the pure excitement of a narrative that makes your heart race and your imagination soar. They don't just write books. They create experiences that make readers feel alive.

THE FOREST

Writing begins as an act of vulnerability for Forest authors. It's not about telling a story so much as revealing a piece of oneself, creating a landscape where readers don't just visit, but become permanent residents of a deeply personal world.

Serena understood this intimately. Her bookshelves weren't organized by genre, but by the emotional landscapes they represented. Each book was a universe unto itself, connected by invisible threads of her unique perspective. Where other writers saw boundaries between genres, she saw opportunities for connection.

Their worlds are constructed not from external research or market trends, but from the rich internal terrain of personal experience. Their writing transcends genre. A Forest author might write a murder mystery, a sweet romance, and a speculative fiction novel that all feel fundamentally different yet unmistakably connected by a singular voice.

This isn't about narcissism. It's about authenticity. A Forest writer's superpower lies in their ability to inject their unique perspective into every narrative, creating a shared language that transforms readers from passive consumers into active participants in a collaborative storytelling experience.

In fiction, this means creating characters that feel less like fictional constructs and more like extensions of the author's own complex inner world. These characters don't just move through a plot. They embody different facets of human experience, filtered through the author's distinctive lens of understanding. When a reader says, "This feels like something only [Author] could have written," they're acknowledging the Forest writer's true gift.

Non-fiction becomes equally personal. A Forest writer doesn't simply present information. They weave personal narrative, research, and insight into a tapestry that feels both deeply informative and intimately human. Their books become conversations, inviting readers to see the world from a unique perspective rather than presenting a detached, objective view.

The greatest challenge for Forest writers is finding balance. Their natural tendency is to go deep. Sometimes that means going so deep that they risk becoming incomprehensible to readers outside their immediate creative ecosystem. The most successful learn to create entry points, to build bridges that invite readers into their world without overwhelming them.

Serena's breakthrough came when she stopped trying to fit her writing into predefined boxes. She realized her strength wasn't in conforming to genre expectations, but in creating a body of work so distinctively her own that genres became irrelevant. Her readers didn't follow her because of a specific type of story, but because of her way of seeing the world.

This approach requires remarkable creative courage. Forest writers must be willing to be vulnerable, to expose the intricate emotional landscapes that drive their storytelling. They create not just books, but entire universes of meaning, inviting readers to see the world through a lens both deeply personal and universally resonant.

Their writing becomes a bridge between individual experience and collective understanding. Where other ecosystems might see writing as a product or a trend, Forest writers see it as a living, breathing entity, constantly evolving, constantly revealing new layers of human complexity. They don't just write books. They create worlds where readers can discover new ways of understanding themselves.

THE AQUATIC

Imagine storytelling not as a linear process of writing a book, but as an expansive ecosystem of narrative experiences. This is the world of the Aquatic writer who sees stories not as static objects, but as living, breathing universes waiting to be explored.

Maya's studio looked nothing like a traditional writer's workspace. Storyboards covered the walls, interconnected with colored strings. Prototypes of game pieces sat alongside manuscript drafts. Concept art for potential film adaptations leaned against shelves filled with books, scripts, and world-building documents. She wasn't just writing a story. She was constructing an entire universe.

Aquatic writers understand that a story is no longer confined to the printed page. Where other writers see a book as an endpoint, Aquatics see it as a beginning, the first invitation into a much larger experience.

In fiction, this means creating narratives so rich and multidimensional that they naturally expand beyond traditional storytelling formats. Consider how George Lucas didn't just write Star Wars. He created an entire mythology that could be experienced through films, books, comics, games, and countless other media. Each format doesn't just supplement the story; it reveals new dimensions of the universe.

Non-fiction becomes equally immersive. An Aquatic writer doesn't simply share information. They design comprehensive learning experiences. Their books are gateways to entire ecosystems of knowledge, complete with complementary online courses, interactive workshops, community platforms, and multimedia resources that transform passive reading into active engagement.

The core of the Aquatic approach is understanding fan experience. These writers don't just create for an audience. They create *with* them. Every narrative decision considers how fans might interact with the story, how they might expand and explore the universe being constructed. It's a collaborative process where the boundary between creator and audience becomes wonderfully blurred.

This approach requires a remarkable breadth of skills. An Aquatic writer must be part author, part game designer, part brand manager, and part community builder. They need to understand not just storytelling, but user experience, transmedia storytelling, and the intricate dynamics of fan engagement.

Maya's latest project began as a science fiction novel but quickly evolved. There was a book, yes, but also a serialized podcast exploring backstory, an augmented reality game that allowed fans to explore the novel's world, and a planned tabletop RPG that would let fans create their own narratives within her universe.

The greatest risk for Aquatic writers is spreading themselves too thin, trying to create so many experiences that the core narrative loses its coherence. The most successful learn to create a strong, central vision that can naturally expand into multiple formats without losing its essential character.

This isn't about marketing or commercial strategy, but lies in understanding storytelling as a fundamentally interactive, expansive experience. An Aquatic writer doesn't just tell a story. They create a world that readers can inhabit, explore, and ultimately make their own.

Their books become invitations to step into entire universes of imagination. They don't just write stories. They build worlds that breathe, grow, and transform with every reader's interaction.

FINDING YOUR LITERARY ECOSYSTEM

Writing is not a singular, uniform path, but a vast landscape with multiple terrains, each offering its own unique possibilities for creative expression. The Author Ecosystems framework reveals that there is no universal "right" way to write—only the way that most authentically resonates with your individual creative spirit.

Each Author Ecosystem represents a distinct approach to storytelling, a unique lens through which writers can understand their creative impulses. These aren't rigid categories, but fluid frameworks that help writers recognize their natural strengths and navigate their creative journey.

The Desert writer understands storytelling as a strategic dialogue with reader expectations, crafting narratives that feel simultaneously familiar and fresh. They are the market navigators, able to quickly identify and respond to emerging literary currents. When the wind shifts to a new trend, they will shift, too, content in writing for any audience, as long as they are entertained.

Grassland writers are the deep-root systems of literature, cultivating comprehensive worlds of understanding. Their approach is about depth, patience, and a commitment to exploring complex ideas with meticulous care. They don't just write stories but grow entire ecosystems of knowledge.

Tundra writers are the performance artists of storytelling, understanding that a book is more than a collection of pages. It's an experience. They stack narrative elements with precision, creating works that generate excitement and sweep readers into immersive journeys.

Forest writers transform storytelling into an act of personal revelation. Their strength lies in their ability to inject a unique perspective into every narrative, creating shared languages that invite readers into deeply personal universes of meaning.

Aquatic writers see storytelling as world-building, creating expansive narrative experiences that transcend traditional media. They understand that a story is no longer confined to a book, but can bloom into multiple formats, inviting interactive engagement.

No Author Ecosystem is better or worse than another. Each offers unique strengths and represents a valid approach to creative expression. We know successful authors in every ecosystem. The key is understanding your natural tendencies, embracing them, and learning how to leverage them most effectively.

Successful writers often evolve, incorporating elements from different Ecosystems as they grow. A Desert writer might develop the depth of a Grassland, a Forest writer might learn the strategic approach of a Desert. The boundaries are fluid, the possibilities endless.

Your writing journey is not about fitting into a predetermined mold, but about discovering the creative landscape that allows your voice to flourish most authentically. It's about understanding that your unique way of seeing the world is not a limitation, but your greatest creative asset.

ENNEAGRAM ARCHETYPES

Enneagrams offer writers something far more profound than simple personality typing. They are a map of human motivation, a lens that reveals the hidden landscape of human desire, fear, and transformation.

Imagine human personality not as a static set of traits, but as a dynamic system of motivation and growth. The Enneagram presents nine fundamental ways humans experience and interact with the world, each driven by a core fear and a core desire that shapes every decision, every relationship, every moment of conflict and connection.

If you want to read more about Enneagrams for Authors, Claire Taylor wrote two great books about this topic in *Reclaim Your Author Career* and *Sustain Your Author Career*. I find the Enneagram to be the best system (outside of ours) to help authors grow, and it happens to be a great framework for designing characters as well.

THE NINE ENNEAGRAM TYPES

1. **The Perfectionist (*The Reformer*)** - *Core Fear:* Being corrupt, bad, or wrong *Core Desire:* To be good, ethical, and right

2. **The Helper (*The Giver*)** - *Core Fear:* Being unwanted or unloved *Core Desire:* To be loved and appreciated
3. **The Achiever (*The Performer*)** - *Core Fear:* Being worthless or failing *Core Desire:* To be successful and admired
4. **The Individualist (*The Romantic*)** - *Core Fear:* Having no unique identity *Core Desire:* To be authentically themselves
5. **The Investigator (*The Thinker*)** - *Core Fear:* Being overwhelmed or incompetent *Core Desire:* To be competent and knowledgeable
6. **The Loyalist (*The Questioner*)** - *Core Fear:* Being without support or guidance *Core Desire:* To feel secure and supported
7. **The Enthusiast (*The Adventurer*)** - *Core Fear:* Being trapped or in pain *Core Desire:* To be satisfied and content
8. **The Challenger (*The Protector*)** - *Core Fear:* Being controlled or vulnerable *Core Desire:* To protect themselves and others
9. **The Peacemaker (*The Mediator*)** - *Core Fear:* Conflict and loss of connection *Core Desire:* To maintain peace and harmony

CHARACTERS THROUGH THE ENNEAGRAM

Every character is a complex ecosystem of motivation, fear, and potential. The Enneagram provides a sophisticated map for understanding how these internal systems operate, revealing characters not as static constructs, but as dynamic psychological landscapes.

Consider Type 1 (The Perfectionist). Their internal world is governed by an unrelenting desire for integrity and correctness. This isn't mere stubbornness, but a deep psychological mechanism designed to avoid corruption. A Type 1 character doesn't simply follow rules. They are driven by an internal moral code so precise, it becomes both their greatest strength and most significant limitation.

In narrative, this might manifest as a character who becomes a whistleblower, not for external recognition, but because the very idea of remaining silent feels like a fundamental betrayal of their core self. Their arc isn't about becoming perfect, but about understanding that imperfection is not the same as moral failure.

A Type 4 (The Individualist) experiences the world as an emotional terrain of profound depth and uniqueness. Their fundamental drive is to understand and express their authentic self, even if that means feeling fundamentally different from everyone else. A Type 4 character brings a rich emotional complexity to a narrative, constantly negotiating between their desire for unique expression and their fear of being misunderstood.

Their narrative journey might involve a creative pursuit where their initial isolation becomes the very source of their artistic breakthrough. The transformation comes not from fitting in, but from discovering that their perceived difference is actually their most powerful creative asset.

The Type 8 (The Challenger) operates from a fundamental need to protect themselves and others. Their external toughness is a carefully constructed defense mechanism protecting a deep vulnerability. A Type 8 character doesn't just display strength; they are constantly negotiating between their protective instincts and their capacity for genuine emotional connection.

In a narrative, this might look like a character who appears confrontational but is actually creating safety for those around them. Their arc involves learning that true strength isn't about control, but about empowerment.

A Type 6 (The Loyalist) lives in a constant negotiation with uncertainty. Their internal system is designed to anticipate and manage potential threats. This isn't paranoia, but a sophisticated survival mechanism. A Type 6 character brings a remarkable capacity for strategic thinking, constantly mapping potential scenarios and preparing for multiple outcomes.

Their narrative journey often involves discovering that their preparedness isn't about avoiding risk, but about developing genuine internal courage. The transformation happens when they learn to trust their own capacity to handle uncertainty.

The Enneagram reveals that characters are not defined by what they do, but by the complex psychological systems driving their actions. Each type represents a unique way of experiencing and responding to the world—a specific set of motivations, fears, and potential growth paths.

This isn't about reducing characters to simple categories. It's about understanding the profound complexity of human motivation. A truly compelling character doesn't just act—they reveal an entire ecosystem of psychological experience.

The most sophisticated characters are those who reveal the intricate dance between limitation and potential. They show us that growth isn't about eliminating our fundamental fears, but about understanding how those fears have both protected and constrained us.

PLOT THROUGH THE ENNEAGRAM

Every plot is a journey of psychological confrontation, and the Enneagram provides a profound framework for understanding how different types experience and navigate narrative challenges.

For a Type 1 (The Perfectionist), a plot becomes a moral crucible. The narrative arc will inevitably challenge their fundamental need for correctness and order. Their story isn't about external victory, but about learning that imperfection isn't inherently wrong. The plot will create scenarios that force them to confront their rigid internal standards, revealing that growth often happens in the messy spaces between right and wrong.

A Type 3 (The Achiever) experiences plot as a series of performance challenges. Their narrative will constantly test the mask of success they've constructed. The most compelling stories for this type create scenarios that strip away external achievements, forcing them to discover value beyond performance. Their transformation comes when they learn that their worth isn't determined by external validation.

Type 4 (The Individualist) experiences the plot as an emotional landscape of profound depth. Their narrative journey is about authenticity—finding a way to express their unique inner world without becoming completely isolated. The most powerful plots for a Type 4 create scenarios that challenge their sense of being fundamentally different, revealing that true individuality comes from connection, not separation.

Type 6 (The Loyalist) experiences plot as a navigation of security and threat. Their narrative arc is fundamentally about confronting fundamental fears. The most interesting stories for this type create scenarios that force them to discover internal courage, to find safety not in external systems, but in their own capacity to handle uncertainty.

Type 8 (The Challenger) experiences plot as a series of tests of strength and vulnerability. Their narrative journey is about learning that true power isn't about controlling others, but about protecting and empowering them. The plot becomes a mechanism for revealing their capacity for genuine leadership and emotional depth.

The Enneagram reveals that the plot is never just about external events. It's a psychological pressure system designed to expose each type's fundamental limitations and potential for growth. Each narrative becomes a unique journey of transformation, carefully calibrated to challenge the specific psychological defenses of the character's type.

A Type 5 (The Investigator) might experience a plot as an intellectual challenge, a journey of understanding that forces them to move beyond observation into actual engagement. Their narrative arc becomes about discovering that knowledge isn't just about collecting information, but about connecting with the world.

The most sophisticated plots don't simply present obstacles. They create precise psychological scenarios that force characters to confront the very mechanisms that have both protected and limited them. Each plot becomes a kind of psychological surgery, carefully designed to expose internal fault lines and create the possibility of genuine transformation.

This is the true power of narrative through an Enneagram lens: Stories become more than sequences of events. They become explorations of human potential, carefully constructed journeys that reveal how we might grow beyond our fundamental limitations.

A plot is not something that happens to a character. A plot is a transformative system designed to reveal the deepest possibilities of human experience.

CONFLICT THROUGH THE ENNEAGRAM

Conflict is the heartbeat of storytelling, but it's rarely as simple as good versus evil or hero versus obstacle. The Enneagram reveals conflict as a complex psychological dance, where each character's fundamental fears and desires create intricate patterns of tension and resolution.

Understanding conflict through the Enneagram means recognizing that every confrontation is a deeply personal negotiation of core psychological needs. Each type approaches conflict with a unique set of strategies, defense mechanisms, and underlying motivations.

TYPE 1 (THE PERFECTIONIST): CONFLICT AS A MORAL CRUCIBLE

For a Type 1, conflict is fundamentally about principle. Their internal landscape is governed by a strict moral code, making every confrontation a potential threat to their sense of righteousness. Conflict for a Type 1 isn't about winning, but about maintaining integrity.

When challenged, they don't simply defend their position. They defend their understanding of what is right. Their most profound conflicts emerge when they're forced to confront the possibility that their rigid standards might be limiting rather than liberating. The narrative tension comes from their struggle between maintaining perfect control and accepting the inherent messiness of human experience.

A Type 1 might become a whistleblower, not for personal gain, but because staying silent feels like a moral compromise. Their conflict is internal as much as external as they are in a constant negotiation between their desire for perfection and the reality of human complexity.

TYPE 2 (THE HELPER): CONFLICT AS EMOTIONAL NAVIGATION

Conflict for a Type 2 is deeply emotional, often revolving around issues of love and rejection. Their greatest fear is being unwanted, which transforms every conflict into a potential threat to their sense of connection.

Their confrontations are rarely direct. Instead, they navigate conflict through emotional manipulation, trying to make themselves indispensable. The narrative tension emerges from their struggle between genuine care and a desperate need to be needed. A Type 2 character might sabotage a relationship to prevent potential rejection, creating conflict through their attempts to avoid it.

TYPE 3 (THE ACHIEVER): CONFLICT AS PERFORMANCE

For a Type 3, conflict is a stage where they must prove their worth. Their fundamental drive is to be seen as successful, which means every confrontation becomes an opportunity to demonstrate their value.

The most compelling conflicts for a Type 3 strip away their carefully constructed image of success. They're forced to confront the difference between their performed self and their authentic identity. Their narrative tension comes from the moment when external achievements can no longer mask their internal insecurities.

TYPE 4 (THE INDIVIDUALIST): CONFLICT AS EMOTIONAL DEPTH

Conflict for a Type 4 is a profound emotional exploration. They don't just experience confrontation. They dive into its emotional complexity, seeing each conflict as an opportunity to understand their unique identity.

Their most significant conflicts emerge from feeling misunderstood. A Type 4 character might intentionally create dramatic situations to feel more deeply, to prove their emotional distinctiveness. The narrative tension comes from their constant negotiation between wanting to be seen and fearing complete exposure.

TYPE 5 (THE INVESTIGATOR): CONFLICT AS INTELLECTUAL CHALLENGE

For a Type 5, conflict is an intellectual battlefield. Their approach is analytical, seeking to understand rather than to win. Their greatest fear is being overwhelmed, so they use knowledge as a defensive mechanism.

Narrative tension for a Type 5 comes from forcing them out of observation and into actual engagement. Their conflicts are often an internal struggle between their desire to understand and their fear of being drained by emotional involvement.

TYPE 6 (THE LOYALIST): CONFLICT AS SECURITY MANAGEMENT

Conflict for a Type 6 is fundamentally about managing potential threats. They're constantly mapping scenarios, preparing for what could go wrong. Their confrontations are strategic, driven by a need to find or create security.

The most compelling conflicts for a Type 6 challenge their need for external support. Their narrative tension emerges from discovering internal courage, learning to trust their own capacity to handle uncertainty.

TYPE 7 (THE ENTHUSIAST): CONFLICT AS AVOIDANCE

For a Type 7, conflict is something to be avoided or reframed as an adventure. Their strategy is to transform potential pain into a positive experience. They're masters of reframing, quick to find the silver lining.

Their most significant conflicts come when they're forced to sit with discomfort. The narrative tension emerges from their struggle to stay present with challenging emotions rather than escaping into possibility.

TYPE 8 (THE CHALLENGER): CONFLICT AS PROTECTION

Conflict for a Type 8 is a direct, powerful expression of protection, both of themselves and others. They meet confrontation head-on, seeing it as a necessary mechanism for maintaining boundaries and ensuring justice.

Their most profound conflicts emerge when they're required to show vulnerability. The narrative tension comes from their journey of understanding that true strength isn't about control, but about genuine connection.

TYPE 9 (THE PEACEMAKER): CONFLICT AS DISSOLUTION

For a Type 9, conflict is something to be dissolved rather than confronted. Their strategy is to merge, to find harmony, often at the cost of their own needs.

Their most significant conflicts are in the internal struggle between maintaining peace and acknowledging their own desires. The narrative tension emerges from their journey toward self-assertion.

THE UNIVERSAL TRUTH OF CONFLICT

The Enneagram reveals that conflict is never just external. It's a complex psychological negotiation, a moment where a character's deepest fears and most profound desires collide.

True narrative tension doesn't come from what happens to a character, but from how a character's fundamental psychological mechanisms respond to challenge. Each conflict becomes an opportunity for transformation, a moment where the character's core limitations are exposed and their potential for growth is revealed.

A story is not about winning or losing. A story is about how we negotiate the complex terrain of our own psychological landscape.

FINDING YOUR CHARACTER'S ENNEAGRAM

Discovering a character's Enneagram type isn't about fitting them into a predetermined box. It's an investigative process of understanding their deepest motivations, fears, and psychological mechanisms. Think of it as a deeply empathetic archaeological dig into the character's inner landscape.

STEP 1: THE FUNDAMENTAL QUESTIONNAIRE

Begin by exploring your character through a series of probing questions:

1. What is their deepest fear?
2. What do they want more than anything else?
3. When they're stressed, how do they typically respond?
4. What do they most want to hide about themselves?
5. What motivates them to get out of bed in the morning?
6. What would completely devastate them if lost?

These aren't surface-level inquiries. They're designed to excavate the psychological bedrock of your character.

STEP 2: SCENARIO EXPLORATION

Create hypothetical scenarios that reveal core motivations:

- Your character is alone and has complete freedom. What do they choose to do?
- Everything they've worked for is suddenly taken away. How do they respond?
- Someone they deeply respect criticizes them. What's their immediate internal reaction?
- They're given the opportunity to solve a long-standing problem. What approach do they take?

These scenarios aren't about what they would do externally, but about understanding the internal process driving their choices.

STEP 3: DEFENSE MECHANISM MAPPING

Every Enneagram type has specific defense mechanisms—psychological strategies they use to protect themselves from fundamental fears:

- Type 1 will try to control and perfect their environment
- Type 2 will attempt to make themselves indispensable
- Type 3 will perform whatever they think means success
- Type 4 will seek unique emotional experiences
- Type 5 will retreat into intellectual understanding
- Type 6 will strategize and prepare for potential threats
- Type 7 will reframe challenges as opportunities
- Type 8 will assert control and protection
- Type 9 will seek harmony and avoid conflict

Watch how your character naturally protects themselves when threatened.

PRACTICAL EXERCISE: CHARACTER ENNEAGRAM DISCOVERY

- Write a free-form monologue in your character's voice
- Do not think about Enneagram types
- Simply let the character speak
- Review the monologue and look for:
    - Repeated emotional patterns
    - Core concerns
    - Fundamental worldview
    - How they speak about themselves and others

WARNING SIGNS OF MISTYPING

- Trying to make the character fit a type
- Focusing on surface behaviors instead of core motivations
- Ignoring the character's complexity
- Forgetting that types are fluid, not fixed

Remember that an Enneagram type is not a limitation, but a starting point for understanding. Your character is not defined by their type, but by how they negotiate their type's inherent challenges and potentials.

The Enneagram is not a scientific classification system, but a sophisticated map of human psychological experience. It offers writers a profound tool for understanding the complex inner worlds of their characters. True character creation happens in the space between understanding and imagination. The Enneagram provides a framework, but the magic occurs when you breathe unique life into that framework.

Your characters are not their types. They are the ongoing story of how they move beyond their initial psychological programming telling a story of how they grow, transform, and discover themselves through the crucible of narrative experience. Using Enneagrams, writing becomes an act of profound empathy, a way of understanding the intricate, beautiful complexity of human motivation.

Write Irresistible Books that Readers Devour

UNDERSTANDING THEME

Most writers get caught up debating plot versus character, as if these were the only two choices for driving a story forward. But there's an element that often gets overlooked, one that can transform a merely successful book into one that creates passionate fans who evangelize your work to others: theme.

Let's look at *The Fault in Our Stars* by John Green. On the surface, it's a story about teenagers dealing with terminal illness. The plot is relatively straightforward. You might even call it quiet. There's some romance, some friendship, some tragedy. Nothing revolutionary in terms of story structure. Yet this book became a cultural phenomenon, spawning a successful movie and cementing Green's place as a leading voice in young adult literature. Why? Because its themes of life, death, and what makes a life well-lived resonated so deeply that readers couldn't stop talking about it.

The story works because everything in it serves these themes. When the characters visit Anne Frank's house, it's not just for historical interest or emotional impact. It creates a powerful thematic parallel between Anne, a teenager who left an outsized legacy despite her short life, and the book's protagonists wrestling with similar questions about meaning and mortality. Even small moments like discussions about books or video games tie back to the central question: how do we find meaning in the time we have?

This level of thematic integration doesn't happen by accident. Whether you plan your themes in advance or discover them during writing, understanding how to recognize and strengthen them can dramatically improve your story's impact. More importantly, it can help you build a loyal readership that follows you across multiple books or even different genres.

Think about your own work for a moment. What themes naturally emerge in your stories? Are you writing about justice? Redemption? The tension between individual desires and societal expectations? Once you identify these themes, you can start using them more deliberately to create deeper resonance with readers.

Theme isn't some fancy literary device reserved for academic analysis. It's a practical tool that can guide every aspect of your storytelling. When you're not sure which plot point to choose or how a character should react in a scene, your theme can point you toward the choice that will resonate most strongly with readers. It's like having a compass that always shows you the most emotionally satisfying direction for your story.

There are generally two paths to working with theme. The first is intentional. You decide upfront what your story is about on a deeper level and build everything else around that foundation. The second is organic. You write the story first, then recognize and strengthen the themes that naturally emerged during the process. Both approaches can work, but there's a catch: the sooner you become aware of your theme, the more effectively you can use it.

BUILDING CONFLICT FROM BELIEF

The most powerful way the theme manifests in your story is through your characters' contrasting worldviews. Instead of thinking about the theme as a message you're delivering, consider it a question your story explores from multiple angles, with each major character representing a different perspective on that central question.

Game of Thrones provides a masterclass in this approach. At its core, the story explores themes of power, like what it means to have it, what it costs to keep it, and how it affects those who wield it. Every major character represents a different philosophy about power, and their conflicts arise naturally from these competing perspectives.

Ned Stark believes power flows from honor and duty. Littlefinger sees it as something to be gained through manipulation and clever maneuvering. Cersei believes in raw force and intimidation. Daenerys tries to balance conquest with compassion. None of these perspectives are entirely wrong. They're all valid approaches to power that create natural conflict when they clash.

This approach works in any genre. Let's say you're writing a mafia romance where your theme explores justice, specifically the tension between law and personal moral codes. You might start thinking your mafia boss love interest should be the villain, but when you dig deeper into the theme, you realize he's fighting for justice too. He's just doing it outside the formal legal system. Meanwhile, your seemingly heroic police chief might be deeply corrupt, using the law to serve personal interests rather than justice. The theme gives you a framework for creating complex characters whose conflicts emerge naturally from their different perspectives on the same core issue.

The key is making sure these contrasting worldviews feel authentic rather than forced. You're not writing characters to prove a point, but instead you're exploring different facets of your theme through their experiences and choices. In *The Hunger Games,* Katniss and Snow aren't just the protagonist and antagonist - they represent fundamentally different views on survival and what people will do to ensure it. Their conflict works because both perspectives emerge naturally from their experiences within the story world.

Character transformation becomes more powerful when it's tied to the theme. Think of character arcs as journeys of thematic understanding. Characters start with one perspective on your theme and, through the events of the story, either evolve toward a more nuanced view or become more entrenched in their initial position. This is where many series writers stumble. They create dramatic character transformations that feel hollow because they're not grounded in the story's themes. True character growth happens when external events force characters to question their fundamental beliefs about your theme.

Consider a romance novel where the theme explores vulnerability and trust. Your protagonist might start believing emotional walls keep you safe, while your love interest believes in taking emotional risks. Their journey isn't just about falling in love. It's about both characters developing a more nuanced understanding of when to guard their hearts and when to open them. The romance works because it serves the theme rather than existing separately from it.

This becomes particularly crucial in series writing. The reason some series maintain reader engagement while others lose steam often comes down to thematic character development. Take *Star Wars* as a cautionary tale. The controversy around *The Last Jedi* wasn't just about plot choices. Most of the hate came because it fundamentally violated how the series had previously explored its themes about heroism and legacy. While the movie might have worked as a standalone meditation on these themes, it broke the thematic trust established with audiences over multiple films.

Contrast this with how *The Dresden Files* handles character development across multiple books. The protagonist's growing power creates increasingly complex moral challenges, but these challenges all explore the series' core themes about responsibility and the corrupting nature of power. The external threats get bigger, but more importantly, they force deeper engagement with the established themes.

When developing characters, ask yourself how each one views your central theme. What experiences shaped their perspective? How do their beliefs about the theme influence their decisions? What would it take to change their mind? These questions often lead to more interesting character choices than simply asking what they want or fear.

The most compelling antagonists usually arise from this thematic approach. Instead of creating villains who oppose your protagonist just to create conflict, develop characters whose perspective on your theme naturally conflicts with your protagonist's view. This creates antagonists who feel real because their opposition comes from genuine belief rather than plot necessity.

Remember that characters can engage with your theme in both subtle and dramatic ways. Not every character needs to represent an extreme position. Sometimes the most interesting thematic tensions come from characters who mostly agree but differ on crucial details. Think about how different friends might agree on a broad principle but argue passionately about its application. These nuanced conflicts often feel more authentic than stark philosophical oppositions.

DRIVING PLOT THROUGH DEEPER MEANING

Once you understand how a theme works through character, you can start using it to drive your plot in more meaningful ways. Rather than just creating events that sound exciting, you can develop plot points that naturally emerge from thematic tension. This makes your story feel more cohesive and gives readers a deeper emotional investment in what happens.

The best plot twists aren't just surprising. They force characters to confront their beliefs about your theme in new ways. In a murder mystery, the most satisfying reveal isn't just about who did it, but challenges everything the protagonist believed about justice or truth.

Consider how *The Hunger Games* handles plot development. When Katniss volunteers for her sister in the first book, it's not just an inciting incident, but also represents our first glimpse of how personal love conflicts with systemic oppression. The games themselves aren't just action sequences. They're explorations of how different characters respond to survival pressure. Even the love triangle works thematically because each potential partner represents a different philosophy about how to respond to war and violence.

This approach becomes particularly crucial when writing series. Many writers struggle with escalating stakes across multiple books, falling into the trap of making each threat bigger than the last until they've written themselves into a corner. Just look at what happened with *The Vampire Diaries*. They kept raising the stakes with bigger and bigger supernatural threats until they had to completely reset the story to make it manageable again.

A more sustainable approach is to deepen your thematic exploration rather than just raising external stakes. In *Anne of Green Gables,* the external stakes remain largely the same throughout. Anne Shirley is navigating life in Avonlea throughout, but the emotional depth of the series grows with her. Initially, her conflicts are about proving herself: winning over Marilla and Matthew, excelling in school, and taming her impulsive nature. As she matures, the stakes shift inward. The question is no longer whether she belongs, but how she reconciles her dreams with reality, learns to deal with loss, and ultimately defines success and love on her own terms. By the time Anne makes peace with staying in Avonlea and choosing a future with Gilbert, it feels earned because we've followed her emotional evolution from an imaginative, insecure orphan to a self-assured woman who understands that happiness isn't about chasing grand adventures but embracing the life she has built.

Russell Nohelty

Every scene in your book should either explore your theme directly or show its impact on your characters. This doesn't mean every scene needs to be heavy with meaning. Sometimes theme appears in subtle ways through character choices, dialogue, or even setting details. In *The Fault in Our Stars,* even quiet scenes like playing video games or reading books work because they're not just about the activities. They're about how different characters find purpose and connection in their limited time.

Action scenes benefit particularly from thematic grounding. Physical conflicts become more engaging when they're also moments of thematic conflict. A fight scene isn't just about who wins. It's about what the fight means within your story's larger thematic framework. This is why training montages in sports movies work so well - they're not just about getting stronger, they're about the theme of personal growth and transformation.

When plotting your story, try asking yourself how each major event challenges or reinforces your characters' beliefs about the theme. What situations would force them to either defend their perspective or question it? What developments would create natural conflict between characters with different thematic viewpoints? These questions often lead to plot points that feel both surprising and inevitable - the hallmark of satisfying storytelling.

Series writers should pay particular attention to how their plot developments serve their themes. The last thing you want is to find yourself in book six with plot threads that have nothing to do with your core thematic concerns. This doesn't mean every subplot needs to directly address your theme, but they should all connect to it in some way. Think of your theme as the trunk of a tree - subplots can branch out in different directions, but they all need to connect back to that central support.

Some of the most effective plots work by gradually revealing different aspects of your theme. Each plot development shows readers a new angle on the central thematic question, building toward a deeper understanding rather than just increasing external tension. This approach can help you maintain reader engagement even in quieter moments because they're still discovering new facets of your theme.

THEME AS STORY ENGINE

Once you understand how your theme works through character, you can start using it to drive your plot in more meaningful ways. Rather than just creating events that sound exciting, you can develop plot points that naturally emerge from thematic tension. This makes your story feel more cohesive and gives readers a deeper emotional investment in what happens.

The best plot twists aren't just surprising. They force characters to confront their beliefs about your theme in new ways. In a murder mystery, the most satisfying reveal isn't just about who did the deed it challenges everything the protagonist believed about justice or truth. In romance, the darkest moment of the story, when the characters turn away from each other, works best when it strikes at the heart of what the characters believe about love. This isn't just about creating drama - it's about making those dramatic moments meaningful within your story's larger thematic framework.

In *The Song of Achilles,* every scene either directly explores or subtly reinforces its central theme: the tension between love and fate. Even seemingly quiet moments—like Achilles and Patroclus training together, telling stories, or simply resting in each other's presence—carry emotional weight because they illustrate their growing bond and the looming inevitability of destiny. These small, tender interactions aren't just filler; they highlight how love shapes their choices and how, despite their attempts to find happiness in the present, the shadow of Achilles' prophesied fate is always present. By the time the tragic conclusion arrives, it feels all the more devastating because every moment leading up to it has been infused with the story's core theme.

THEME AS MARKETING TOOL

Understanding themes becomes even more crucial when you start thinking about marketing your work and building a lasting author brand. Traditional publishing has long recognized books with strong thematic cores because these books tend to create passionate readers who become long-term fans. As independent authors, we need to understand this same principle.

Think about how readers talk about books they love. They rarely just describe the plot. Instead, they focus on how the book made them feel, what it made them think about, how it changed their perspective. These reactions all stem from the theme. When readers say they "felt seen" while reading your book, what they're really saying is that your thematic exploration resonated with their own experiences and beliefs.

Marketing becomes much clearer when you understand your theme. If you're writing a mafia romance that explores justice outside the law, that's a more compelling pitch than just "it's about a mafia boss and the woman who loves him." If your cozy mysteries explore how small communities handle moral compromises, that's more interesting than just "amateur sleuth solves crimes." Theme gives readers a deeper reason to pick up your book beyond just genre conventions.

Consider how the theme influences reader targeting. Different themes naturally appeal to different reader groups. A theme about finding belonging might resonate particularly with young adult readers. Themes about second chances often connect with older romance readers. Understanding these connections helps you position your work more effectively and find your ideal audience.

Theme becomes particularly powerful for series marketing. When readers connect with your thematic exploration, they're more likely to follow you through multiple books. Look at how Melanie Harlow handles this - she can reposition the same book for different audiences by emphasizing different thematic elements. During the holidays, she might highlight themes about family and tradition. During summer, she might emphasize themes about personal transformation. The story doesn't change, but the thematic focus shifts to match reader interests.

Your theme can also help differentiate your work in crowded genres. Let's say you're writing paranormal romance. Instead of just saying, "It's vampires," you can position it based on your unique thematic approach. Are you exploring addiction through vampire bloodlust? The cost of immortality on human connection? The tension between power and love? These thematic angles help your work stand out while attracting readers who specifically connect with your thematic interests.

Author branding becomes clearer when you understand your themes. John Green and his brother Hank have built strong author brands precisely because readers know what thematic territory they explore. Even when working in different genres, their consistent thematic interests create a recognizable brand. This is particularly powerful for Forest type writers who might work across multiple genres. For them, their theme becomes the thread that ties their work together.

But theme-based marketing requires honesty. You need to actually deliver the thematic experience you're promising. If you position your book as a deep exploration of redemption but treat that theme superficially, readers will feel misled. This is where understanding how to develop themes through character, plot, and world-building becomes crucial - it helps you create stories that fulfill the promises your marketing makes.

Social media marketing becomes more effective when you understand your themes. Instead of just promoting plot points or romance tropes, you can share content that connects to your thematic interests. If your books explore themes about found family, sharing content about friendship and chosen connections will resonate with your ideal readers. If you write about justice and corruption, commenting on related real-world issues (thoughtfully and appropriately) can build audience connection.

Theme also influences how you handle your backlist. Understanding the themes that run through your work helps you package and promote older books effectively. You might bundle books with similar thematic explorations, even if they're in different genres. You could create reading orders based on thematic progression rather than just publication date. Theme gives you more marketing options beyond simple genre categorization.

Remember that theme-based marketing isn't about being pretentious or literary. It's about understanding what makes your stories emotionally satisfying and communicating that to potential readers. Even "simple" genres like action thrillers or cozy mysteries have themes that resonate with readers. The key is identifying those themes and learning to talk about them in ways that connect with your audience.

Most importantly, a theme helps build sustainable careers. When readers connect with your thematic interests, they're more likely to become long-term fans who anticipate each new release. They'll follow you across genres and formats because they trust you to deliver the kind of emotional and intellectual experience they're seeking. By creating deep thematic connections with readers who share your interests and concerns, you can build a career that lasts beyond individual books or series.

Russell Nohelty

CREATING CHARACTERS

In our previous chapters, we explored how to develop compelling ideas and weave strong themes through your work. Now we turn to what might be the most crucial element of any story: the characters who bring those ideas and themes to life. While a great concept might draw readers in, it's the characters who keep them turning pages late into the night.

Think about the last story that truly grabbed you. Chances are, you weren't just invested in what happened, but were also invested in who it happened to as well. The most brilliant plot twist means nothing if readers don't care about the characters affected by it. The most thought-provoking theme falls flat if readers can't see it embodied in characters they connect with.

This is why understanding character development isn't just about crafting interesting personalities. It's about creating the engine that drives your entire story forward. When done well, your characters become the living embodiment of your themes, the catalyst for your plot developments, and the emotional anchor that keeps readers invested through every twist and turn.

Consider how *The Hunger Games* succeeds not just because of its high-concept premise, but because Katniss

Everdeen embodies the story's themes about survival, sacrifice, and systemic oppression. Every time she faces a choice between self-preservation and helping others, she's not just advancing the plot - she's exploring the story's central themes through her actions. Her internal struggle with isolation and connection mirrors the larger thematic exploration of individual versus collective survival.

But what makes certain characters "stick" with readers while others fade from memory? The answer often lies in their "core wounds" that we talked about earlier that make characters feel real and relatable even in fantastical situations. These aren't just backstory elements. They're the emotional engines that drive character decisions and development throughout the story.

Take Jon Snow from *Game of Thrones*. His core wound centers on shame and legitimacy, stemming from his status as a bastard. This isn't just background information - it influences every major decision he makes, from joining the Night's Watch to his later choices about power and leadership. Even when he's doing heroic things, the underlying wound colors his motivations and internal struggles.

What's particularly interesting is how these core wounds often reflect the author's own thematic interests. Many successful authors, especially those working in longer series, find themselves returning to similar thematic territory because they're exploring their own core wounds through different character perspectives. This isn't a weakness. It's often what gives their work its distinctive voice and emotional authenticity.

The key is understanding that characters serve multiple functions in your story:

- They embody and explore your themes through their actions and choices
- They provide emotional connection points for different types of readers
- They create natural conflict through their contrasting worldviews
- They drive plot through their decisions rather than having plot happen to them

BUILDING CHARACTERS FROM THE INSIDE OUT

The most memorable characters aren't defined by their surface traits but by their inner worlds. While physical descriptions and personality quirks can make a character distinctive, it's their psychological makeup that makes them unforgettable. Understanding how to build characters from the inside out starts with recognizing the power of core wounds and psychological triggers.

A Core Wound isn't just backstory. It's the psychological injury that shapes how your character sees and interacts with the world. For Jon Snow in *Game of Thrones,* his identity as a bastard isn't just a fact about his birth. It's a deep wound of shame that influences every relationship he forms and every decision he makes. Even when he rises to positions of power, that underlying sense of being an outsider colors his perspective and choices.

These core wounds often fall into recognizable categories that resonate deeply with readers: abandonment, betrayal, rejection, shame, powerlessness, or injustice. The universality of these experiences is what allows readers to connect with characters even in fantastical situations. A reader might never face an army of ice zombies, but they understand Jon Snow's struggle with feeling like an outsider trying to prove his worth.

Layering the Enneagram system on top of this provides a particularly useful framework for understanding how to shape engaging personality. For instance, Type Eight characters, like many thriller protagonists, are driven by a core wound around control and vulnerability. Their outward strength often masks a deep fear of being controlled or hurt by others. This creates natural internal conflict when the plot forces them to trust or depend on others.

Consider Katniss Everdeen from *The Hunger Games.* Her core wound centers on abandonment and the burden of responsibility shaped by losing her father and having to become the provider for her family at a young age. This wound manifests in her difficulty trusting others and her instinct to handle everything alone. Throughout the series, the plot continuously challenges this tendency by putting her in situations where she must learn to trust and work with others to survive.

What makes her character particularly effective is how her actions often contradict her conscious beliefs. While she thinks of herself as a lone wolf, her actual choices repeatedly demonstrate care for others, like volunteering for her sister, allying with Rue, trying to protect Peeta. This tension between her wound-driven belief system and her true nature creates compelling internal conflict that drives both character development and plot.

The key to using core wounds effectively is understanding that they create false belief systems that your character must eventually confront. A character wounded by betrayal might believe they can never trust anyone, leading them to push away potential allies. A character wounded by powerlessness might believe they must maintain absolute control, causing them to make decisions that ultimately harm their relationships. These false beliefs create natural obstacles for your character to overcome.

This is where the character arc intersects with the theme. The journey of confronting and moving beyond these false beliefs often embodies your story's central thematic concerns. In *The Crown*, Queen Elizabeth's story explores power and duty through her struggle between personal desires and royal responsibility. Her character arc isn't just about learning to be a good queen - it's about exploring what power and duty mean on both personal and societal levels.

When developing your characters, start by identifying their core wound and the false beliefs it has created. Then consider:

- How does this wound influence their current behavior and choices?
- What situations would force them to confront their false beliefs?
- How do their relationships challenge or reinforce their wound-driven behavior?
- What would healing or growth look like for this character?

Don't feel limited to a single wound or psychological trigger. The most compelling characters often carry multiple wounds that create complex internal dynamics. In romance, the "alpha male" character type often combines wounds around control and vulnerability with wounds around trust or worthiness. This layering creates more opportunities for character development and emotional resonance with different readers.

Remember, core wounds don't have to be dramatic or traumatic to be effective. Sometimes the most relatable characters carry everyday wounds, including the need to prove their worth, the fear of being truly seen, or the struggle to balance personal desires with responsibilities. What matters is how these wounds shape the character's worldview and choices in ways readers recognize from their own experiences.

THE HEART OF STORY CONFLICT

Characters don't exist in isolation. They come alive through their interactions with others. The most compelling stories often emerge not from external events but from the complex web of relationships between characters with different worldviews, wounds, and ways of approaching life's challenges.

Consider how *Friends* approaches this dynamic. Each main character represents different aspects of personality and different approaches to life's challenges. Monica's need for control plays against Phoebe's free-spirit nature. Joey's emotional openness contrasts with Chandler's defensive humor. When these characters interact, their different approaches to life create natural conflict and comedy without requiring external plot devices. The show succeeds because these personality dynamics feel authentic and create natural story opportunities.

This principle works across genres. In *The Hunger Games,* Katniss's relationships reveal different aspects of her character while exploring the story's themes. Her protective relationship with Prim shows her capacity for sacrifice. Her complicated dynamic with Peeta challenges her tendency toward emotional isolation. Her friendship with Rue forces her to confront the human cost of the games. Each relationship serves both character development and thematic exploration.

The key to creating effective character relationships lies in understanding how different worldviews and core wounds interact. When characters have opposing approaches to life's fundamental questions, conflict arises naturally from their interactions. A character who believes in taking risks will naturally clash with one who prioritizes security. A character wounded by betrayal will struggle to trust even loyal allies.

Game of Thrones masterfully demonstrates this principle through its sprawling cast. Each major house represents a different philosophy about power and leadership. The Starks believe in honor and duty. The Lannisters prioritize family legacy and cunning. The Targaryens claim divine right through bloodline. When these philosophies clash, they create compelling conflicts that drive the story forward while exploring deeper themes about the nature of power and governance.

But effective character dynamics aren't just about conflict. They're also about growth and transformation. The most powerful relationships in stories often involve characters who challenge each other's core wounds and false beliefs. In romance, this often manifests as characters whose strengths address each other's weaknesses. The guarded character meets someone who teaches them to trust. The character who fears vulnerability encounters someone who shows them the strength in opening up.

This is where the concept of character foils becomes crucial. A foil isn't just a character who contrasts with your protagonist - they're someone who specifically challenges your protagonist's worldview or core beliefs. In *Pride and Prejudice,* Darcy isn't just Elizabeth's love interest - he's someone whose presence forces her to confront her own prejudices and assumptions. Their relationship works because they challenge each other's flaws while respecting each other's essential nature.

When developing relationships between characters, consider:

- How do their core wounds and beliefs interact?
- What can they learn from each other?
- How do their differences create natural conflict?
- What aspects of your theme do their interactions explore?

Remember that character relationships should evolve over time. Static relationships quickly become boring. Look for ways to challenge and change established dynamics through plot events and character growth. When *The Crown* depicts the relationship between Queen Elizabeth and Princess Margaret, it shows how their sisterly bond evolves and strains under the weight of royal duty. The changing nature of their relationship reflects the series' larger themes about power, duty, and personal sacrifice.

BEYOND BASIC TROPES

Understanding character archetypes isn't about following formulas. It's about recognizing patterns that resonate with readers and knowing how to adapt them for modern audiences. Every genre has its traditional character types, not because writers lack imagination, but because these patterns speak to fundamental human experiences and expectations.

In thriller fiction, we typically see two dominant patterns. Generally, the protagonist is either the hypercompetent professional facing their greatest challenge, or the ordinary person thrust into extraordinary circumstances. Think of Jason Bourne versus the protagonist of *The Da Vinci Code*. Both types can work brilliantly, but they serve different narrative purposes and appeal to different reader fantasies. The hypercompetent protagonist fulfills our desire for mastery and control, while the ordinary person thrust into danger lets readers imagine how they might rise to similar challenges.

Romance offers particularly clear examples of how archetypes evolve with social changes while maintaining their core appeal. The "alpha male" character type has evolved significantly from its origins. Modern romance writers often maintain the surface traits of strength and capability but add crucial elements of emotional intelligence and respect for boundaries. The "alpha" isn't just physically powerful - they're emotionally mature enough to be vulnerable with their chosen partner while maintaining healthy boundaries with others.

Similarly, the "hot mess heroine" archetype speaks to readers' experiences with imperfection and growth. These characters aren't just chaotic. They're usually competent in some areas while struggling in others, reflecting real-world experiences of trying to balance different life aspects. Their journey often involves not just finding love but finding self-acceptance, which resonates with readers facing similar challenges.

In fantasy, traditional archetypes like the chosen one or the wise mentor persist because they embody fundamental human experiences of discovering inner strength and seeking guidance. But modern fantasy often subverts these tropes in interesting ways. Instead of the mentor being all-knowing, they might be flawed or uncertain. The chosen one might reject or struggle with their destiny rather than embracing it immediately.

The key to working with archetypes effectively lies in understanding the emotional needs they serve. Take the "found family" trope common in fantasy and science fiction. This archetype resonates because it speaks to universal desires for belonging and acceptance while offering the possibility of choosing one's own support system. Shows like *Firefly* succeed by giving each crew member a distinct role in the family dynamic while exploring how these relationships help heal individual wounds.

Different genres handle character complexity differently. In romance, complexity often comes through layering multiple tropes. A character might embody both the "grumpy one" and the "caretaker" archetypes, creating interesting tension between their prickly exterior and nurturing core. This layering makes characters feel more realistic while still fulfilling genre expectations.

Thriller and mystery writers often create complexity through professional competence contrasting with personal struggles. The brilliant detective might solve impossible cases while failing to maintain personal relationships. This contrast humanizes characters while maintaining their genre appeal.

Fantasy and science fiction frequently build complexity through cultural and social dynamics. A character might embody traditional hero traits while struggling with systemic injustice or competing loyalties. This allows writers to explore contemporary themes through fantastical settings.

When working with archetypes, consider:

- What emotional need does this character type typically fulfill for readers?
- How can you maintain that core appeal while adding fresh elements?
- What aspects of the archetype might feel dated or problematic for modern readers?
- How can you layer multiple archetypes to create more complex characters?

The most successful modern characters often combine elements from different archetypal traditions. *Bridgerton* demonstrates this by merging historical romance archetypes with contemporary sensibilities about agency and consent. The characters feel period-appropriate while addressing modern readers' expectations about relationships and personal growth.

Remember that archetypes exist because they work. The goal isn't to avoid them entirely but to understand why they resonate and how to make them feel fresh for contemporary audiences. Even highly original characters usually share DNA with established archetypes - they just combine or subvert these elements in interesting ways.

CHARACTERS AS THE HEARTBEAT OF STORYTELLING

Characters are more than just names on a page or actors moving through a plot. They are the living, breathing embodiment of a story's deepest truths. They are the vessels through which readers explore complex emotional landscapes, confront universal human experiences, and ultimately make sense of the world around them.

The best main characters, even if the main character is you, are the ones who become avatars for the reader's transformation and can make them feel like they are the hero.

Relationships become the crucible in which characters are truly revealed. The most dynamic stories populate their worlds with characters who challenge, complement, and transform one another. In *Game of Thrones*, characters like Daenerys and Jon Snow aren't just individuals. They're reflections of different approaches to power, leadership, and personal transformation. Their interactions reveal deeper truths about the story's themes of duty, survival, and systemic oppression.

Genre plays a crucial role in character development, each offering unique opportunities for exploring human complexity. Romance allows for deep emotional vulnerability, showing characters breaking through their protective walls. Thrillers test characters' competence and moral boundaries. Fantasy provides space for profound personal transformation against epic backdrops. The best stories, regardless of genre, understand that external adventures are meaningful only insofar as they reveal internal landscapes.

As we prepare to dive into world-building in the next chapter, remember that settings are more than mere backdrops. They are the stages upon which these carefully crafted characters will dance their intricate emotional journeys. A world gains depth and meaning through the characters who inhabit it, revealing their struggles, their hopes, their fundamental humanity.

For writers, the challenge is not just to create characters, but to create characters so authentically human that readers see themselves reflected in the story's emotional truth. It's about understanding that every character carries a universe within them—complex, contradictory, and endlessly fascinating.

In the end, great characters are not about perfection, but about authenticity. They are about showing the beautiful, messy process of how we struggle, how we fail, and how we ultimately transform. They remind us that every story, no matter how fantastical, is fundamentally a story about what it means to be human.

As we turn the page to explore the worlds that will house these remarkable characters, remember: a truly great world is not defined by its geography or magic systems, but by the characters whose lives will unfold within it.

THREE METHODS FOR BUILDING CHARACTER RELATIONSHIPS

At the heart of every great novel lies not just compelling ideas, but a carefully orchestrated cast of characters whose interactions drive the story forward. Understanding how to structure these character relationships is crucial for turning your initial concept into a fully realized narrative.

The foundation of any strong novel is the main character. *Without a protagonist who captures both the writer's and readers' imagination, even the most intriguing plot will fall flat.* This character becomes the linchpin around which the entire story revolves. However, it's in the careful orchestration of relationships between characters that a story truly comes to life.

There are three approaches I use to structure character relationships, each offering distinct advantages for different types of stories.

The first is **the Triangle Method,** exemplified brilliantly in *The Matrix*. Consider how the story centers on Neo as the protagonist, with Trinity and Morpheus as the two crucial supporting characters. Each brings essential elements to the narrative: Morpheus provides guidance and wisdom, challenging Neo's understanding of reality, while Trinity offers emotional connection and represents faith in Neo's potential. These aren't merely secondary characters, but carefully crafted complements to the protagonist, each illuminating different aspects of Neo's journey from confused programmer to humanity's savior.

Russell Nohelty

What makes this triangular relationship structure particularly effective is how it enables multiple narrative threads to develop simultaneously. When Neo trains in the construct, Morpheus can be investigating potential threats, while Trinity monitors the real world. By separating these three main characters periodically, the story explores different aspects of its world while maintaining momentum.

What makes the Triangle Method particularly effective is how it enables multiple narrative threads to develop simultaneously. By separating these three main characters periodically, allowing them to pursue individual investigations or journeys, the story can explore different aspects of its world or plot while maintaining narrative momentum.

A key principle here is to generally keep no more than two of these main characters together at any time, bringing all three together primarily to share discoveries and advance the overall plot.

The second approach is the ***Ensemble Method,*** exemplified by works like *One Hundred Years of Solitude*. This more complex structure involves roughly six main characters who can be mixed and matched in various combinations. Think of how García Márquez weaves together the various generations of the Buendía family, each combination revealing new aspects of both the characters and the story's themes. Each pairing creates unique dynamics while moving the plot forward in unexpected ways.

While this method offers rich possibilities for character development and interweaving plotlines, it requires careful management to prevent the story from becoming unwieldy. For first-time novelists especially, handling more than six main characters can quickly become overwhelming. Even *The Three-Body Problem,* which eventually expanded to a massive cast, began with a more focused approach before broadening its scope.

The third approach, **the Linear Journey Method**, is often the most straightforward and therefore particularly effective for newer writers. Consider *The Alchemist,* where Santiago moves through his journey encountering various supporting characters – the king of Salem, the crystal merchant, the Englishman – each serving specific narrative purposes before the story moves on. ***While these supporting characters might reappear throughout the narrative, they don't require the same depth of development as main characters in the other approaches***, as they exist primarily to facilitate the protagonist's journey toward a final confrontation or goal.

Think of this method as creating a string of pearls, where each supporting character represents a pearl the protagonist encounters along their journey. While some of these characters might be vitally important to the story, perhaps even as memorable as the protagonist themselves, they don't necessarily need to undergo their own character arcs or have extensive viewpoint scenes.

The choice between these three methods should be guided by your story's needs and your own strengths as a writer. The Linear Journey Method often proves most manageable for first novels, while the Triangle Method offers a good balance between complexity and manageability. The Ensemble Method, while powerful, typically requires more experience to execute effectively.

Remember that regardless of which method you choose, every character should serve a purpose in revealing or developing aspects of your protagonist, advancing the plot, or illuminating themes in your story.

Even in an ensemble piece, characters shouldn't exist merely to populate your world. They should each contribute meaningfully to the narrative tapestry you're weaving.

CREATING MAIN CHARACTERS AND VILLAINS

Once you have a framework for how your characters will interact, the next crucial step is developing those characters themselves. Let's explore a fundamental approach to character development through the lens of *The Matrix*, which offers an excellent study in character dynamics and development.

Every compelling character starts with a foundation of three positive traits, three negative traits, and both external and internal goals.

This simple framework provides the core from which deeper character development can grow. Let's examine Neo, our ***protagonist***, through this lens.

His positive traits include his innate curiosity about the nature of reality, his willingness to sacrifice himself for others, and his unrelenting determination. His negative traits manifest as self-doubt, a tendency toward isolation, and initial reluctance to embrace his destiny. These traits drive his actions throughout the story and make him relatable despite the extraordinary circumstances he faces.

But what truly brings a character to life is the interplay between their internal and external goals. Neo's external goal is straightforward. He wants to understand what the Matrix is and later to save humanity from machine dominion. However, his internal goal runs deeper: he seeks self-understanding and authenticity in a world of illusions. This tension between external and internal motivations creates the rich character development that drives the story forward.

The creation of a compelling *antagonist* is equally crucial, and Agent Smith serves as a masterclass in villain development. The best villains are not simply evil for evil's sake. They are the heroes of their own story and often serve as a dark mirror of the protagonist. Smith's positive traits include his efficiency, his dedication to purpose, and his intelligence. His negative traits manifest as his contempt for humanity, his obsession with control, and his inability to accept change.

What makes Smith such a compelling antagonist is how he reflects Neo's own journey in a twisted way. Both characters begin to question their reality and their purpose. While Neo's questions led him toward embracing human potential and free will, Smith's led him toward a desire to destroy what he sees as the virus of human existence. Both characters evolve beyond their original programming, but they make radically different choices with that freedom.

This mirroring between hero and villain creates deep thematic resonance. Both Neo and Smith are, in essence, programs trying to transcend their coding – Neo as a human breaking free from the Matrix's control, Smith as an agent breaking free from his programmed purpose. The key difference lies in their response to this freedom: Neo uses it to protect others, while Smith uses it to destroy what he cannot control.

SUPPORTING CHARACTERS

The supporting characters, Morpheus and Trinity, further complement and challenge Neo's character development.

Morpheus embodies unwavering faith and wisdom, serving as a guide but also representing a kind of certainty that Neo must both learn from and ultimately transcend. Trinity represents both strength and vulnerability, challenging Neo's tendency toward isolation by offering both emotional connection and practical support.

When developing your own characters, remember that this mirroring and complementary relationship between characters creates the tension and dynamics that drive compelling narratives. Your protagonist's traits should be challenged and illuminated by both your antagonist and supporting characters, creating a web of relationships that adds depth to your story's themes and conflicts.

The key is to ensure that each character, while serving the larger narrative, remains the hero of their own story.

Even minor characters should have clear motivations that make sense from their perspective. This approach creates a richer, more believable world where conflicts arise not from arbitrary evil, but from genuine, understandable, yet opposing desires and beliefs.

Building on our discussion of character relationships in *The Matrix*, it's helpful to understand how different types of characters serve distinct narrative functions. We can borrow useful terminology from video games to understand these roles more clearly - specifically the concepts of "NPCs" (Non-Player Characters) and "boss characters."

In *The Matrix*, while Neo, Trinity, and Morpheus form our core triangle, and Agent Smith serves as our primary antagonist, the story is enriched by numerous other characters who serve different narrative purposes. **Think of the Oracle as a quintessential "NPC" - she doesn't directly oppose Neo but rather provides crucial information and guidance that moves his journey forward.** She presents him with choices and insights that help him understand his path, much like the Grail Knight in Indiana Jones who helps guide the hero toward their goal without serving as an obstacle.

Tank and Dozer serve similar NPC functions. They're not adversaries to overcome, but rather supporting characters who help propel the story forward through their knowledge, assistance, and contributions to Neo's journey. The same could be said for Switch and Apoc, who, while more minor characters, each contribute to moving the plot forward in their own ways.

In contrast, characters like Agent Jones and Agent Brown function as "boss" characters, intermediate antagonists that Neo must overcome on his way to the final confrontation with Agent Smith. The Merovingian in the sequels is another example of a boss character, an obstacle that must be overcome to progress the story, but not the ultimate antagonist.

Understanding these different character functions helps us create richer narratives. Your NPCs should each serve a distinct purpose in moving your protagonist's journey forward, whether through information, guidance, or support. They might test your protagonist, but their primary role is to aid development rather than oppose it. Meanwhile, your boss characters provide escalating challenges that help demonstrate your protagonist's growth while building toward the ultimate confrontation with the main antagonist.

This layered approach to character functionality - from core relationships, to antagonists, to supporting characters both helpful and hostile - creates the depth and complexity that makes stories resonate with readers. Each character type serves its own crucial purpose in the larger narrative machinery, contributing to both plot progression and character development in distinct but complementary ways.

The most resonant stories understand a fundamental truth: none of this is about you, the writer, or even your characters. Every scene, every choice, every emotional beat exists solely as a vehicle for reader transformation. Your protagonist's journey is merely the lens through which readers process their own potential for change.

Consider how Katniss Everdeen's story works not because we care deeply about her personal fate, but because her growth from survivor to revolutionary speaks to every reader's desire to move beyond mere existence toward meaningful impact. The character's specific circumstances matter less than how they illuminate universal paths to transformation.

When you give precise language to universal struggles, like the weight of responsibility, the fear of being truly seen, the yearning for connection, readers recognize their own unspoken experiences. This recognition creates what we call "emotional resonance" - the moment when readers think "Yes, that's exactly how it feels." The more accurately you can name these shared human experiences, the more deeply readers will connect with your story.

This is why effective characters should be clear windows, not detailed portraits - defined enough to carry the story, yet transparent enough that readers can project their own struggles and aspirations onto the journey. Your job isn't to tell your story or even your character's story. It's to craft an experience that gives voice to what readers have always felt but perhaps never had words to express.

Remember: readers don't actually care about your characters. They care about what those characters reveal about their own lives and potential for transformation. The true power of a story lies not in clever plots or complex characters, but in your ability to articulate the universal human experiences that connect us all.

Russell Nohelty

WORLD-BUILDING

"All fiction is world-building," Gina Bianchini observed during a discussion in our community about story last year. This simple statement reveals a profound truth that many writers overlook. Whether you're crafting an epic fantasy realm or a small-town romance, you're creating a world that must feel both familiar enough to enter and fresh enough to explore. The most successful authors understand that world-building isn't just about creating elaborate magic systems or detailed maps. It's about crafting an environment so compelling that readers want to live there, even long after they've finished the book.

After establishing your core characters and their relationships, the next crucial element of creating a hooky story that sells books is crafting the world they inhabit. However, it's essential to understand that world-building should flow from character, not the other way around. Your world exists to challenge and test your characters, creating the perfect environment for their story to unfold.

Consider how *The Matrix* masterfully structures its world-building around Neo's journey. The film begins in what we might call the "starting world", which is the familiar reality of late 20th century urban life. This world serves several crucial functions: it establishes the status quo, introduces the basic rules of reality as the characters (and audience) understand them, and most importantly, shows us Neo in his familiar environment before everything changes.

This **starting world** perfectly sets up both Neo's internal and external conflicts. Internally, he feels disconnected from this reality, sensing something fundamentally wrong with the world - his famous "splinter in the mind." Externally, his hacker activities and encounters with Trinity begin to pull him toward the truth. ***The starting world becomes increasingly unstable as these internal and external pressures mount***, eventually becoming untenable when agents come for Neo at his workplace.

The film then moves us through what we might call a **transition world**, made up of the initial scenes after Neo takes the red pill. This space serves as a buffer zone between the familiar starting world and the harsh reality of the "real world." In this transition, both Neo and the audience learn the new rules gradually. The construct program where Morpheus explains the nature of reality, followed by Neo's awakening in the real world, provides a crucial learning period before the full dangers of the new world must be confronted.

This structural approach to world-building is particularly effective because even in its most "out there" moment, only about 10-20% of your world should be completely unfamiliar to your audience.

Even in a story as reality-bending as *The Matrix*, most elements remain recognizable. Office politics, the feel of city streets, human relationships and emotions are all things we see in our everyday life. The truly foreign elements, the nature of the Matrix, the technology of jacking in, the physics-defying abilities, are introduced gradually, building upon familiar foundations.

Time frame also plays a crucial role in making your world digestible. *The Matrix* primarily takes place over a relatively compressed timeframe, which helps the audience process the radical changes in Neo's understanding of reality. When dealing with complex world-building, a tighter timeframe often helps readers or viewers maintain their grasp on the story's events and implications.

Let's examine how this escalation of world-building works in *The Matrix*:

1. **Starting World:** The familiar "real" world, which we later learn is the Matrix
2. **Destabilization:** Strange events and encounters begin to erode Neo's sense of reality
3. **Transition World:** The construct program and initial awakening in the real world
4. **New World:** The full reality of the human-machine war and the nature of the Matrix

Each stage builds upon the previous one, ***never*** overwhelming the audience with too much new information at once. Even when revealing the most fantastic elements of its world, *The Matrix* anchors them in recognizable human experiences and emotions - the universal feelings of questioning reality, seeking truth, and fighting for freedom.

This methodical approach to world-building serves the story's central character journey. Every aspect of the world exists to challenge Neo's understanding of reality and force him to confront his own potential. The world isn't complex for complexity's sake; its complexity serves the character's development and the story's themes.

THE TWO STANDARD DEVIATIONS RULE

One of the most common mistakes writers make is trying to present too much world-building too quickly. Brandon Sanderson articulates what we call the Two Standard Deviations Rule, which states that your world should never be more than two steps removed from what readers already know and understand. Think of it like leading someone through an unfamiliar house at night. You want to keep one hand on the familiar while reaching for something new.

Consider how *Game of Thrones* introduces its world. George R.R. Martin begins with something readers can grasp immediately: medieval-style political intrigue based on the War of the Roses. The supernatural elements, like the White Walkers, the dragons, and the magic, come later, after readers are firmly grounded in the human dynamics of this world. When Martin does introduce magical elements, he does so gradually, allowing readers to acclimate to each new aspect while maintaining their connection to the story's core human drama.

This principle applies equally to contemporary settings. Lucy Score's *Knockemout* series demonstrates this beautifully in how it builds its small-town world. Rather than overwhelming readers with every detail of the town at once, Score introduces key locations that become characters in their own right: the women-run restaurant where the staff's cycles have synced, creating both humor and conflict; the barbershop that serves as a community hub where crucial information flows. These places feel real because they're grounded in familiar experiences while offering unique twists that make them memorable.

Successful world-building often follows what we might call the "iceberg principle". Readers should sense that there's much more beneath the surface than what they initially see. However, you don't need to show them the entire iceberg at once. In fact, you shouldn't.

The Mandalorian exemplifies this approach perfectly. The show begins with familiar *Star Wars* elements. They are a mysterious bounty hunter, a frontier-like setting, recognizable technology. But with each episode, it peels back layers of its world, revealing new aspects of Mandalorian culture, the post-Empire political landscape, and the complex relationships between different factions. This gradual unveiling keeps viewers engaged while never overwhelming them with too much information at once.

Similarly, in Melanie Harlow's romance series, the town of Cloverleigh Farms reveals itself gradually through multiple books. Each story focuses on a different couple, but also illuminates new aspects of the community, its history, and its interconnections. By the end of the series, readers have a rich, detailed understanding of the setting, but they've acquired this knowledge naturally through character experiences rather than through exposition dumps.

CREATING ACCESSIBLE ENTRY POINTS

The key to effective world-building lies in creating clear entry points for readers, including familiar elements that help them understand and connect with your world before you introduce more exotic or complex aspects. This is why portal fantasy has been so consistently successful as a subgenre. Works like *The Chronicles of Narnia* use the "normal" world as a launching pad into fantasy, allowing readers to discover the magical realm alongside protagonists who share their frame of reference.

But this principle extends far beyond fantasy. Consider how *The Crown* approaches its historical setting. While most viewers aren't familiar with the inner workings of the British monarchy, the show begins by focusing on relatable human elements—a young woman facing unexpected responsibilities, family dynamics, relationship challenges. The complex political and historical aspects are introduced gradually, always anchored in these more universal experiences.

Contemporary romance author Elana Johnson demonstrates this principle in her small-town series by starting with a protagonist who's new to the community. This outsider perspective allows readers to discover the town's quirks, traditions, and unwritten rules naturally, without feeling lost or overwhelmed. The protagonist's journey of integration into the community mirrors the reader's process of understanding and investing in the world of the story.

A crucial aspect of the Two Standard Deviations Rule is understanding that "familiar" doesn't mean "boring." In fact, starting with familiar elements allows you to build deeper, more nuanced worlds because readers have a solid foundation for understanding how your world differs from their own.

The Expanse demonstrates this brilliantly in its science fiction setting. Rather than immediately diving into complex space opera elements, it begins with a noir detective story, which is a familiar genre for many readers. The science fiction elements are introduced gradually, each building on established understanding. Political tensions between Earth, Mars, and the Belt mirror historical colonial relationships, making complex interplanetary politics accessible through familiar patterns.

Even in contemporary settings, this principle helps create richer worlds. In her *Knockemout* series, Lucy Score builds on familiar small-town elements. Everyone knows everyone else's business, local businesses serve as community hubs, town festivals and traditions. But she uses these familiar elements as a foundation for introducing unique aspects of her world, like the complex relationships between different social groups or the town's particular brand of justice.

COMMON PITFALLS TO AVOID

Understanding the foundation of world-building also means recognizing common mistakes that can disconnect readers from your world. Here are several crucial pitfalls to avoid:

1. **The Information Dump**: Resist the urge to explain everything about your world upfront. Readers don't need, and usually don't want, to know every detail immediately. Focus on what's relevant to the current story moment. The more you parse out your world over time, the better you can avoid this trap.

2. **Complexity Without Purpose:** Every aspect of your world should serve your story somehow. *The Vampire Diaries* demonstrates what happens when world-building becomes too complex. By the later seasons, they had introduced so many supernatural elements and rules that they had to essentially reset the story to make it manageable again.

3. **Inconsistency:** Once you establish how something works in your world, maintain consistency. This doesn't mean you can't reveal new aspects, but they should align with what's already been established. *Game of Thrones* maintains consistency in its magic system by establishing early that magic has costs and limitations, then building on these principles rather than contradicting them.

4. **Forgetting the Human Element:** No matter how fantastical your world, readers connect through human experiences and emotions. *The Hunger Games* works not because of its dystopian setting alone, but because it grounds that setting in Katniss's very human struggles and relationships.

5. **Neglecting Sensory Details:** A world becomes real through specific, concrete details that engage the senses. *The Gilded Age* brings 1880s New York to life not just through historical facts, but through rich sensory details, like the rustle of silk dresses, the clatter of carriages on cobblestones, the contrast between old money mansions and new money ostentation.

By understanding and applying these foundational principles, you create a world that readers can enter gradually and naturally, becoming more invested with each new revelation. Remember that your goal isn't to create the most unique or complex world possible, but to craft a setting that serves your story and engages your readers fully in the experience you're creating.

CHARACTERS AS WORLD-BUILDERS

A world remains lifeless until we experience it through the eyes, hearts, and minds of compelling characters. The most elaborately constructed setting will fail to engage readers if they don't have a meaningful lens through which to discover and explore it. This is why successful world-building is inextricably linked to character development. Your characters aren't just inhabiting your world, they're revealing it to readers through their experiences, relationships, and conflicts.

The "fish out of water" trope persists across genres because it provides such an effective framework for world revelation. When we follow characters discovering a new environment, whether it's a small town, a fantasy realm, or a complex social hierarchy, their learning process mirrors and guides the reader's understanding. Consider how *The Chronicles of Narnia* uses Lucy's first steps through the wardrobe to introduce readers to its magical world. Her wonder, confusion, and gradual understanding help readers process and accept each new fantastical element they encounter.

This technique works equally well in contemporary settings. In Lucy Score's *Knockemout* series, the first book introduces the town through Naomi, a newcomer whose outsider perspective allows readers to discover the community's quirks and characteristics naturally. Her reactions to the town's unique elements, like the synchronized cycles of the restaurant staff or the informal justice system, help readers understand and accept these aspects of the world while maintaining their engagement with the story.

Characters reveal your world not just through what they're learning, but through what they already know. In *The Hunger Games*, Katniss's detailed knowledge of hunting and foraging does more than establish her character. It reveals crucial information about District 12's desperate conditions and the Capitol's oppressive control. The way she thinks about and uses these skills tells readers volumes about her world without requiring explicit exposition.

This principle applies across genres. Consider how *The Expanse* uses the contrasting knowledge bases of its viewpoint characters to reveal different aspects of its complex solar system civilization. Detective Miller's street-level understanding of life on Ceres Station provides a different perspective than Chrisjen Avasarala's high-level political knowledge, allowing readers to build a complete picture of the world through these complementary viewpoints.

THE POWER OF RELATIONSHIPS

Character relationships provide another crucial avenue for world revelation. When characters interact, their relationships naturally expose aspects of your world's social structure, power dynamics, and cultural norms. *The Gilded Age* demonstrates this beautifully through its exploration of old money versus new money relationships in 1880s New York. The way characters interact across social boundaries reveals more about the period's complex social hierarchy than any amount of direct exposition could achieve.

In fantasy and science fiction, relationship dynamics can illuminate complex world-building elements organically. *The Mandalorian* uses Din Djarin's relationships with other

Mandalorians to reveal the complexities of their culture and belief systems. Different interpretations of "The Way" emerge through character interactions rather than exposition dumps, making the world-building feel natural and engaging.

The most effective character-driven world-building often features characters who embody different aspects of your world's fundamental conflicts or characteristics. *Game of Thrones* exemplifies this approach. Each major house represents different philosophies about power and leadership, allowing the story to explore these concepts through character actions and interactions rather than abstract exposition.

Even in contemporary settings, characters can embody different aspects of your world's central tensions. In Melanie Harlow's romance series, different characters represent varying approaches to traditional values versus modern sensibilities, allowing the stories to explore these themes through personal conflicts rather than social commentary.

A character's internal conflicts can reveal crucial aspects of your world's complexity. In *The Crown,* Elizabeth's struggle between her personal desires and royal duties illuminates the monarchy's demands and restrictions more effectively than any historical exposition. Her internal battles make the world's constraints feel immediate and emotionally resonant rather than merely academic.

Science fiction and fantasy can use this technique particularly effectively. Consider how *The Expanse*'s James Holden's internal conflicts about loyalty and justice reveal the complex political and moral landscape of a solar system divided by competing interests. His personal struggles mirror and illuminate larger systemic issues within the story's world.

As your characters grow and change, their development can parallel and reveal deeper aspects of your world. *The Dresden Files* demonstrates this well. As Harry Dresden gains power and understanding, readers discover new layers of the supernatural world alongside him. His character development becomes a vehicle for expanding the reader's understanding of the world's complexity.

This principle works equally well in contemporary settings. In Lucy Score's series, each protagonist's journey reveals new aspects of *Knockemout*'s community dynamics and values. As characters overcome personal challenges, they also illuminate different facets of the town's character and culture.

COMMON CHARACTER-DRIVEN WORLD-BUILDING MISTAKES

Understanding how characters drive world-building also means recognizing common mistakes that can undermine this relationship:

1. **The All-Knowing Newcomer:** Avoid having characters who are supposedly new to a world but somehow understand all its complexities immediately. *The Mandalorian* avoids this by having Din Djarin learn new aspects of his own culture throughout the series, making the world feel deep and complex.

2. **The Inconsistent Reactor:** Characters should respond to their world's unusual elements consistently based on their background and personality. If a character is amazed by one piece of technology but completely unfazed by another equally extraordinary innovation, it breaks reader immersion.
3. **The Exposition Dump Dialogue:** Avoid having characters tell each other things they would already know just to inform readers. *The Expanse* handles this well by having characters share information only when it's naturally relevant to their immediate situation.
4. **The Static Character in a Dynamic World:** As your world reveals new aspects, your characters should respond and adapt to these revelations. *Game of Thrones* shows this through characters like Sansa Stark, whose understanding and navigation of power evolves as she experiences different aspects of her world.
5. **The Unaffected Observer:** Characters should be shaped by their world's unique characteristics. If your world has specific cultural norms, power structures, or physical laws, these should influence how characters think and behave.

TECHNIQUES FOR CHARACTER-DRIVEN WORLD REVELATION

Characters serve as our most powerful lens for revealing the intricate details of story worlds. Through their experiences, conflicts, and relationships, we can naturally expose the complexities of our settings without relying on exposition. The key lies in treating characters as active participants rather than passive inhabitants of pre-constructed worlds.

Consider how *The Gilded Age* reveals the complex social dynamics of 1880s New York through contrasting character perspectives. By showing both old money and new money viewpoints on the same social situations, the show illuminates class structures, cultural expectations, and power dynamics organically through character interaction. These contrasting perspectives create depth while maintaining reader engagement through emotional investment in the characters' experiences.

Natural information exchange happens most effectively through relationships. A mentor explaining traditions to a newcomer, cultural misunderstandings between characters from different backgrounds, or even casual conversations that reveal societal expectations - all these moments build world understanding while serving character development. When characters react to new elements of their world, readers process and accept these additions through the emotional lens of characters they trust.

The networks of relationships between characters provide another powerful tool for world-building. As characters navigate different social circles, form alliances, and encounter conflicts, they expose various aspects of your world's structure and dynamics. A character moving between high society and working-class environments naturally reveals class distinctions. A forbidden romance illuminates cultural taboos and expectations.

Most importantly, character growth should parallel world revelation. As characters develop and change, their evolving perspective allows readers to discover new layers of world complexity. A character who begins in a limited social position but gains power and influence can expose readers to increasingly complex aspects of political or social systems. Their personal transformation becomes a vehicle for deeper world understanding.

Remember that every character interaction, reaction, and development creates opportunities to deepen readers' understanding while maintaining their emotional investment in the story. When characters actively engage with their world rather than simply existing within it, readers discover that world through authentic human experience rather than abstract description.

THE FRAMEWORK OF YOUR WORLD

Every world, whether magical or mundane, operates according to systems and rules. These aren't just constraints. They're the framework that makes your world feel real and allows for meaningful conflict and resolution. Understanding how to create and reveal these systems effectively can transform your world-building from mere setting description into a dynamic force that drives your story forward.

Brandon Sanderson's *First Law of Magic* provides a crucial insight that extends far beyond fantasy: the ability to solve problems with your world's systems should be directly proportional to how well readers understand those systems. This principle applies whether you're writing about magic spells, advanced technology, or social hierarchies.

In *The Expanse,* the rules of space travel and physics represent a hard system. They're clearly defined, consistent, and crucial to problem-solving. When characters need to navigate dangerous situations, their understanding of these physical laws determines their success or failure. The rules about how ships move, how gravity works, and how space affects the human body create both opportunities and limitations that drive the story.

Contrast this with *The Crown*'s portrayal of royal protocol and political influence, which is a soft system where the rules are more fluid and open to interpretation. While there are clear guidelines about how the monarchy should function, the real drama comes from how characters navigate the grey areas and unwritten rules. The system is soft enough to allow for surprise and adaptation while maintaining enough structure to create meaningful stakes.

Sanderson's Second Law states that limitations are more interesting than powers. This principle extends beautifully beyond fantasy and science fiction. In *The Good Place,* the afterlife's point system creates clear limitations that drive conflict and character development. The rules aren't just arbitrary restrictions. They also force characters to grapple with fundamental questions about morality and personal growth.

Even in contemporary romance, limitations create compelling dynamics. In Lucy Score's *Knockemout* series, the small town's social systems and unwritten rules create boundaries that characters must either respect or deliberately choose to cross. These limitations generate natural conflict and force characters to make meaningful choices about how they'll operate within or challenge the established order.

Every system should have associated costs and consequences. In *The Mandalorian,* the dedication to "The Way" comes with significant personal and practical costs for Din Djarin. His adherence to Mandalorian customs creates both advantages and complications, making his choices about when to bend these rules meaningful.

The Gilded Age demonstrates how social systems carry implicit costs and consequences. Characters must constantly weigh the benefits of social advancement against the price of achieving it. Every choice to conform to or challenge social expectations carries specific consequences that affect both individual characters and their relationships.

BUILDING CONSISTENT SYSTEMS

Creating consistent systems within your world requires careful attention to how different elements interact and evolve. Like a living ecosystem, every aspect of your world should influence and respond to other parts in logical, coherent ways. Consider how *Game of Thrones* weaves together its political, economic, and magical systems. A change in one area, like the return of dragons, creates rippling effects through political power structures and economic relationships, making the world feel authentically complex while remaining comprehensible.

The scale of your systems should align naturally with your story's scope. *The Hunger Games* built systems that work at both personal and societal levels. Individual choices, like Katniss's decision to volunteer, connect meaningfully to larger systemic conflicts. The games themselves function as a microcosm of broader social dynamics, allowing readers to understand complex societal issues through intimate personal drama.

Systems must also be able to evolve while maintaining internal consistency. *The Expanse* excels at showing how technological and social systems adapt to new discoveries and challenges. As humanity expands through the solar system, both technology and society change in response to new environments and opportunities. Yet these changes follow established rules, making them feel natural rather than arbitrary.

Revealing these systems effectively requires subtlety and patience. Rather than explaining how things work, show characters encountering system limitations through their failures and struggles. *The Mandalorian* reveals the complexities of Mandalorian culture not through exposition but through moments when Din Djarin confronts the boundaries of his beliefs. These personal conflicts illuminate cultural systems more effectively than any explanation could.

Contrast between characters provides another powerful tool for system revelation. *The Gilded Age* uses the differences between old money and new money perspectives to naturally expose the intricate social rules of 1880s New York. Through their conflicts and misunderstandings, readers grasp complex social dynamics without ever feeling lectured.

Start with fundamental elements and gradually introduce complexity as your story progresses. *The Expanse* begins with basic concepts of space travel before delving into more complex physics and political dynamics. This progressive revelation allows readers to build understanding naturally while maintaining engagement with the story's human elements. Consistent systems create the foundation for believable worlds. When readers understand how your world works - not through explanation but through experiencing its effects on characters - they become more invested in both the story and its consequences.

SYSTEMS ACROSS GENRES

While fantasy and science fiction often have the most obvious systems, every genre benefits from well-constructed frameworks:

ROMANCE

Modern romance novels often operate within multiple overlapping systems:

- Social expectations and dating norms
- Professional hierarchies and workplace rules
- Family dynamics and traditions
- Community standards and relationships

These systems create natural conflict and force characters to make meaningful choices about which rules they'll follow or break in pursuit of love.

MYSTERY/THRILLER

Effective mysteries require clear systems governing:

- Investigation procedures and limitations
- Power structures and jurisdictions
- Information access and verification
- Character relationships and loyalties

The balance between procedural rules and human elements creates tension and drives the story forward.

LITERARY/CONTEMPORARY FICTION

Even literary fiction operates within carefully constructed systems:

- Social hierarchies and class dynamics
- Cultural expectations and traditions
- Family roles and responsibilities
- Professional advancement and achievement

COMMON SYSTEM-BUILDING MISTAKES

Creating consistent systems requires avoiding several common pitfalls that can undermine your world's believability. Think of your story's systems like the laws of physics. They create the fundamental framework within which your characters must operate. Once established, these rules need to remain consistent unless their evolution becomes a central part of your narrative.

Breaking established rules for plot convenience creates "system fractures" where readers lose faith in your world's internal logic. If your magic system explicitly can't raise the dead, having a character suddenly perform resurrection to solve a plot problem shatters the framework you've built. Instead, characters should overcome limitations by deeply understanding and cleverly working within established rules, just as scientists achieve breakthroughs by mastering natural laws rather than ignoring them.

Adding complexity to your systems without purpose often leads to what we might call "world-building bloat" -

intricate rules and mechanisms that don't meaningfully affect your story. Consider how *The Expanse*'s complex physics matters because it directly shapes character choices and creates plot tensions. Every detail of how ships maneuver and how gravity affects human bodies generates both problems and opportunities that drive the story forward.

Perhaps most crucially, systems need meaningful limitations to create engaging narrative possibilities. A magic system without costs, a society without constraints, or technology without drawbacks rarely generates interesting problems for characters to solve. The most compelling systems balance opportunities with obstacles, giving characters tools to pursue their goals while presenting authentic challenges they must overcome.

Every system in your world should exist to serve your story, creating natural sources of conflict and opportunity that drive character growth and plot development. When readers understand your world's rules, they can fully engage with how characters navigate both the possibilities and limitations these systems present.

PRACTICAL APPLICATIONS

When developing your world's systems, consider these questions:

1. What fundamental rules govern your world's operation?
2. How do these rules create both opportunities and limitations for characters?
3. What costs and consequences are associated with operating within or challenging these systems?

4. How do different systems interact with and influence each other?
5. How will you reveal these systems to readers organically?

BUILDING FLEXIBLE FRAMEWORKS

The most effective world systems provide frameworks that support story development while maintaining enough flexibility for surprise and discovery. *The Mandalorian* demonstrates this balance beautifully. The rules of Mandalorian culture are clear enough to create meaningful conflicts but flexible enough to allow for character growth and unexpected developments.

Remember that your goal isn't to create the most complex or original systems possible, but to build frameworks that support your story's needs while feeling authentic and engaging to readers. Whether you're writing about magical powers, social hierarchies, or professional protocols, your systems should enhance rather than overshadow the human elements that make stories compelling.

The best world systems aren't just rules to be followed. They are dynamic frameworks that generate story possibilities while maintaining enough structure to make choices meaningful. By understanding and applying these principles, you can create worlds that feel both coherent and alive, providing rich territory for character development and story evolution.

THEMATIC INTEGRATION - MAKING YOUR WORLD MATTER

The most powerful worlds aren't just backdrops for action. They're physical manifestations of your story's deeper themes. Every aspect of your world, from its broadest systems to its smallest details, should contribute to the larger ideas you're exploring. When world-building and theme align effectively, the setting becomes an active participant in your story's meaning rather than just a stage for events to unfold.

The Hunger Games provides a masterclass in thematic world-building. The stark contrast between the Capitol's excess and the districts' deprivation doesn't just create visual interest. It physically embodies the story's themes about inequality and systemic oppression. The gaudy fashion and elaborate feasts of the Capitol aren't just setting details; they're physical manifestations of the corruption and moral decay at the heart of society.

This principle works equally well in contemporary settings. In Lucy Score's *Knockemout* series, the small town setting isn't just a backdrop for romance. It's a physical embodiment of themes about community, belonging, and informal justice. The women-run restaurant becomes more than just a location; it represents female solidarity and power in a male-dominated world. The barbershop isn't just a business; it's a symbol of community knowledge and connection.

One of the most powerful techniques in thematic world-building is finding concrete ways to represent abstract concepts. *The Expanse* demonstrates this brilliantly in how it uses the physical realities of space travel and colonization to explore themes of class division and resource inequality. The physical differences between Earth, Mars, and the Belt become tangible representations of social and political divisions.

The Crown uses the physical spaces of palaces and royal residences to explore themes of duty, tradition, and personal sacrifice. The grandiose state rooms versus private apartments become physical manifestations of the divide between public duty and personal life. The very architecture embodies the weight of tradition and expectation that shapes the characters' choices.

Your world's systems and rules should reinforce your themes rather than just creating plot mechanics. In *The Good Place*, the afterlife's point system isn't just a plot device—it's a physical manifestation of questions about morality, personal growth, and what makes a good person. The system's complexity and sometimes contradictory nature reflects the show's larger themes about the challenges of ethical behavior in a complex world.

Game of Thrones demonstrates this principle through its approach to power. The physical Iron Throne, made of melted swords and deliberately uncomfortable, becomes a perfect physical metaphor for the show's themes about the cost and burden of power. The Wall isn't just a defensive structure; it's a physical embodiment of themes about boundaries, duty, and the tension between civilization and chaos.

Effective thematic world-building often employs environmental storytelling by using physical locations and details to reinforce themes without explicit explanation.

The Gilded Age uses the architecture and decoration of different New York homes to explore themes about old versus new money, tradition versus progress, and the performance of social status. Every architectural detail and decorative choice tells a story about its inhabitants' values and aspirations.

The Mandalorian uses this technique through its portrayal of different planets and settlements. Each location's physical characteristics from prosperous ports to struggling frontier towns reinforces themes about survival, community, and the cost of empire. The state of each settlement becomes a visual representation of larger political and social themes.

CHARACTER INTERACTION WITH THEMATIC SPACES

How characters interact with their physical environment should reflect and reinforce your themes. In *The Crown*, Elizabeth's changing relationship with Buckingham Palace mirrors her evolution as a monarch. Her initial discomfort with its grandeur, followed by her growing command of the space, physically represents her journey from unprepared young woman to confident queen.

The Expanse demonstrates this through how different characters move through and adapt to various space environments. Their physical comfort or discomfort in different gravity conditions becomes a metaphor for larger themes about belonging, adaptation, and the human cost of expansion into space.

Contrast is a powerful tool in thematic world-building. *Game of Thrones* uses the stark differences between locations like Winterfell and King's Landing to explore themes about honor versus pragmatism, tradition versus ambition. The physical characteristics of each location reinforce these thematic contrasts.

In contemporary settings, *The Gilded Age* creates similar thematic contrast through its portrayal of old and new money homes. The traditional, understated elegance of old money residences versus the ostentatious display of new money mansions becomes a physical representation of competing social values and approaches to power.

As your story progresses, your world's physical spaces should evolve in ways that reflect thematic development. *The Hunger Games* shows this through the destruction and transformation of various districts throughout the series. These physical changes mirror the transformation of the society and the evolution of themes about revolution and systemic change.

In *The Mandalorian*, the changing state of Mandalorian communities and artifacts reflects evolving themes about cultural identity and adaptation. The physical scattering and gathering of Mandalorian people and resources becomes a tangible representation of themes about cultural preservation and change.

Creating thematic resonance through world-building requires careful attention to how every element of your world reinforces your core ideas. Like a symphony where each instrument contributes to the overall composition, every aspect of your world should harmonize with your central themes. When elements disconnect from these themes, they create narrative discord that pulls readers out of the experience you're crafting.

Heavy-handed symbolism presents another common pitfall in thematic world-building. Consider how *The Hunger Games* builds its critique of systemic oppression through naturally occurring elements of its world. The stark contrast between District poverty and Capitol excess doesn't feel manufactured because it emerges organically from the story's internal logic. The games themselves serve as both plot device and thematic metaphor without ever feeling artificially constructed to make a point.

Your world's physical elements need to maintain thematic consistency unless contradiction itself serves your themes. When your story explores ideas about power and corruption, every aspect of your world should reflect and reinforce these themes. Any contradictions should serve deliberate purpose rather than resulting from inconsistent world-building.

Most importantly, thematic spaces must evolve alongside your themes. As characters grow and themes develop, your world should reflect these changes. A castle that represents oppressive authority at the story's beginning might transform into a symbol of reclaimed power by the end. Static environments suggest static themes, while dynamic spaces reinforce the idea that meaningful change is possible.

Remember that effective thematic world-building creates resonance between setting and story, making your themes feel inevitable rather than imposed. When every element of your world naturally supports your central ideas, readers experience your themes through immersion rather than instruction.

PRACTICAL APPLICATIONS

When developing thematic world-building, consider these questions:

1. What are your core themes?
2. How can physical spaces and details represent these themes?
3. What systems in your world naturally connect to your themes?
4. How can character interaction with the environment reinforce themes?
5. What contrasts in your world help illuminate your themes?

GROWING YOUR UNIVERSE

The art of expanding a fictional world presents one of storytelling's greatest challenges. Whether you're planning a series from the start or responding to unexpected success, understanding how to grow your world sustainably can mean the difference between a satisfying saga and a bloated narrative that collapses under its own weight. The key lies in planning expansion that feels both natural and necessary, serving your story's core rather than merely adding complexity for its own sake.

In N.K. Jemisin's *The Broken Earth* trilogy, the narrative begins with a single mother reeling from personal tragedy in a harsh, quake-ravaged land. At first, the story focuses on her immediate survival and grief, hinting at an entrenched social order that shuns those with magical abilities. As the trilogy unfolds, Jemisin expands on global cataclysms, ancient technologies, and the deeper origins of these powers. Each step logically builds on the last. By the time the characters confront the planet-wide crisis at the heart of their civilization, readers feel each new layer is a natural outgrowth of what has come before, rather than a sudden, arbitrary escalation.

Consider how Julia Quinn's *Bridgerton* series begins by centering on a single couple's courtship yet gradually broadens to include the romantic entanglements of each Bridgerton sibling. Because every new development grows naturally from the family's interactions and the well-defined setting of Regency London, the series's scope expands in a way that feels seamless. Even as high-society gossip intensifies, and layered backstories emerge from hidden scandals to shifting alliances. Each progression remains rooted in the core themes established at the start: love, honor, and the unbreakable bond of family.

Game of Thrones demonstrates this technique masterfully in its early books. While the immediate conflict between the Starks and Lannisters drives the main narrative, Martin simultaneously develops Daenerys's journey in Essos and seeds information about the White Walkers. These secondary and tertiary plotlines eventually grow into major narrative threads, but they feel natural because they've been present from the beginning.

When working with multiple plot threads, consider how they'll evolve across a series. *A subplot in one book might become the main plot of a subsequent book, creating narrative threads that pull readers through your series.* Each subplot should either reach resolution within its book or clearly set up future developments.

The key to making this structure work is maintaining proper pacing within each component. Every sequence should contain two main objectives - a smaller goal achieved around the 5,000-word mark, followed by a larger climactic moment near 10,000 words. Every chapter sets up a new threat or challenge in its opening scene and resolves it (though not necessarily successfully) in its final scene.

We already talked about The Levitz Paradigm to juggle multiple plot lines of varying importance, and it truly comes into its own during this kind of planning.

Managing the scale of your story presents one of the biggest challenges in world expansion, as *The Vampire Diaries* illustrates. As the series progressed, the writers kept introducing bigger supernatural threats and more powerful beings, eventually writing themselves into a corner where they had to essentially reset the story to make it manageable again. *The Mandalorian* offers a contrasting approach to expansion. Rather than constantly escalating the scope of conflicts, the show deepens its exploration of existing elements. New aspects of Mandalorian culture and galactic politics emerge naturally from established foundations rather than through the introduction of ever-more-powerful threats.

Successful world expansion often involves deepening your existing elements rather than simply adding new ones. *The Gilded Age* demonstrates this principle through its exploration of 1880s New York society. Instead of introducing wildly new elements, the show delves deeper into the complexities of established social structures, revealing new layers of meaning and conflict within familiar frameworks. Lucy Score's *Knockemout* series similarly expands by deepening rather than widening. Each book reveals new aspects of the town and its inhabitants, but these revelations emerge from existing relationships and locations rather than through the introduction of completely new elements.

Creating sustainable world expansion requires understanding several crucial elements working in concert. Your world's fundamental aspects must be solid enough to support growth, like a tree with strong roots that can support new branches.

Any expansion should emerge naturally from existing elements, much as *The Expanse* builds its larger conflicts from established scientific and political foundations. These expansions must reinforce rather than dilute your core themes, as *The Crown* maintains its focus on duty, power, and personal sacrifice even as it moves through different historical periods. New elements should connect meaningfully to your characters' development, as *The Mandalorian* introduces new aspects of its world through Din Djarin's personal journey rather than through arbitrary additions.

World expansion looks different across various genres, each presenting unique challenges and opportunities. Fantasy and science fiction authors often find success by deepening their established systems before introducing new ones, ensuring fresh elements connect meaningfully to existing world rules while maintaining consistent costs and limitations.

Romance writers typically expand through relationship networks and community connections, deepening existing locations and social structures while maintaining emotional stakes. Mystery and thriller writers build complexity through interconnected cases or conspiracies, using past events to inform current conflicts while maintaining tension.

The modern storytelling landscape often demands expansion across different media platforms. *The Mandalorian* shows how a world can grow through multiple shows, books, and other media while maintaining consistency. This requires careful attention to fundamental world elements across platforms while taking advantage of each medium's unique strengths. Each piece must stand alone while contributing to the larger world, creating an interconnected universe that rewards engagement across platforms without requiring it.

When building your initial world, consider how it might grow over time. Plant seeds early that could be developed later if needed. Establish world rules flexible enough to allow for expansion while maintaining consistency. Leave certain aspects of your world unexplored but hinted at, creating natural expansion points for the future while adding immediate depth through mystery. Consider how your initial structure can support future development without breaking established rules or feeling forced.

The true measure of successful world expansion isn't found in the quantity of new elements added, but in how meaningfully these additions connect to and enhance what already exists. When you focus on organic growth that serves your story's core elements, you create worlds that continue to engage and surprise readers while maintaining the essential qualities that drew them in initially. Like a well-tended garden, your world should grow in ways that feel both natural and intentional, each new addition contributing to the overall health and beauty of the whole.

Russell Nohelty

PLOT: THE ENGINE OF STORY

The most important thing to understand about structure is that there are all sorts of ways to build it, and everyone seems to have their own twist on it. However, I like to start every story asking, "What are the bones of the story I'm building?"

Plot and structure *can* be the same, but they don't have to be. Think of the movie *Hitman* on Netflix. Even though it is a story about a hitman, it is built on a romantic comedy structure, meaning the two characters had to end up together in the end. If they built it on the bones of a Shakespearean tragedy, then they would have had to die.

The other thing I consider before even starting to outline is the *tone* of the piece. Writing exists on what I call **the Batman to Bugs Bunny parallel**. Tone dictates what can happen in a story. You can't have a slapstick moment in *Batman Begins,* and you can't kill somebody in Bugs Bunny. If you do, you're gonna have a bad time.

Now that we have those bits out of the way, let's actually build our structure. At its highest level, story structure can be broken down into *sequences*, which are substantial chunks of roughly 10,000 words each. Think of these as similar to major sequences in film, with each sequence building to a significant turn or revelation in your story.

For a typical novel of 100,000 words, **you'd be working with ten sequences.** These sequences break down into **chapters,** ideally running between 1,000 and 2,500 words. Each chapter, in turn, contains roughly four scenes, with scenes typically ranging from 250 to 1,000 words. This modular approach to structure creates natural rhythms in your storytelling while helping manage pacing and reader engagement.

What makes this structure particularly effective is how it builds tension. Rather than following the traditional "rising action" model where tension simply escalates linearly, think of it as a series of peaks and valleys, with each peak slightly higher than the last.

In *The Matrix* terms, **Neo doesn't simply get progressively more powerful**. He experiences victories and setbacks, moments of confidence followed by new challenges that reveal how much more he has to learn.

When plotting your story, you don't need to plan every detail in advance. Instead, focus on identifying your major story beats - those crucial moments that must happen to move your story forward. **These become your sequence-level turning points.** The specific path between these points can remain flexible, allowing for creative discovery during the writing process. This combines the benefits of both plotting and "pantsing" (writing by the seat of your pants).

Theme plays a crucial role in holding this structure together. **Your theme influences not just what happens in your story, but how it happens and what it means.** The tone of your work should remain consistent with your theme and inform your structural choices.

For practical purposes, this structured approach allows you to set achievable daily writing goals. *If you can write 250 words (one scene) per hour, you could potentially complete 1,000 words per day.* At that pace, you could finish a sequence every ten days and a complete novel in about three months.

Remember that *while this structure provides a framework, it shouldn't feel constraining.* Think of it as a scaffold that supports your creativity rather than a rigid formula. The goal is to provide enough structure to keep your story moving forward while maintaining the flexibility to explore unexpected directions as they arise.

THE FIRST ACT

The opening act of your story serves as both invitation and promise to your readers. These early chapters don't just introduce your world and characters. They establish the emotional and thematic framework that will support everything that follows. A well-crafted first act creates clear goals that generate conflict and lead to complications that drive the story forward.

Consider how *The Hunger Games* opens. Within the first chapter, we meet Katniss in her ordinary world, understand the brutal reality of the reaping, and witness her life-changing decision to volunteer in her sister's place. This isn't just plot mechanics. It's an elegant demonstration of character building through action. We learn everything we need to know about Katniss through her choices rather than exposition. Her willingness to sacrifice herself reveals her protective nature. Her illegal hunting shows both her practical skills and her willingness to defy authority when necessary. Every detail serves multiple purposes.

The most effective first acts include eight key elements that should be established early:

First, you need to show your protagonist in their ordinary world. This isn't just about setting. It's about establishing both their external circumstances and their internal state. Focus on choosing three key character traits you want readers to associate with your protagonist, then demonstrate those traits through action rather than telling.

Second, explain why today is different. Something must distinguish this day from all others, creating anticipation even before the major inciting incident. In Katniss's case, it's reaping day. For *Game of Thrones*, it's Robert Baratheon coming to demand Ned Stark become the Hand of the King. This preliminary disruption primes readers for bigger changes to come.

Third, include what writing instructor John Truby calls a "ghost", which is the wound or unresolved issue from the past that still haunts your protagonist. This might be shown through memory, conversation, or symbolic representation, but it should hint at the emotional journey ahead.

Fourth, establish opposing groups or forces within the world. These don't have to be obvious antagonists – they might be competing philosophies, social classes, or ways of life. This creates natural tension even before your main conflict emerges.

Fifth, demonstrate either self-sacrifice or self-protection – a moment that shows readers whether to root for or against your protagonist. This is often called the "save the cat" moment, but it can be any action that reveals character through moral choice.

Sixth, reveal your protagonist's fatal flaw, which is the characteristic that will create internal conflict throughout the story. This flaw should be something that makes sense given their background but will need to change for them to achieve their goals.

Seventh, deliver an inciting incident, which is the event that disrupts your protagonist's world and forces them to make a choice. This should be something they can't ignore or avoid without severe consequences.

Finally, show their decision to engage with the conflict, even if they don't fully understand what they're getting into. This commitment moves the story into Act Two and sets up the journey ahead.

The key is making each of these elements serve multiple purposes. A scene showing the protagonist at work isn't just establishing the setting. It's revealing character traits that will become crucial later. The inciting incident doesn't just start the plot. It creates questions that drive reader curiosity. The protagonist's decision doesn't just advance the story; it demonstrates their values and flaws.

Consider how *Game of Thrones* handles these elements in its opening chapters. We see the Stark family's ordinary world at Winterfell, establishing both the physical setting and the values of honor and family loyalty that will drive many character decisions. The arrival of the king's party marks the day as different, while tensions between houses Stark and Lannister establish opposing forces. Ned Stark's execution of the deserter demonstrates both his adherence to duty and foreshadows later conflicts between honor and survival. Each element builds on the others while setting up future developments.

The most common mistake in Act One is trying to explain too much too quickly. Remember that readers don't need to understand everything about your world or characters immediately. They just need enough context to be intrigued by the story's central question or conflict. Focus on creating clear cause-and-effect relationships between events while raising questions that make readers want to know more.

My rule is that you should show the protagonist at home, at work, and at play as early in the book as possible. If you can do it in the first three scenes, then all the better, but once you do that, then you build the bounds of the character in the story. Those three scenes should deal with the character's internal need and external want.

By the end of Act One, readers should understand what's at stake both externally and internally for your protagonist. They should have a sense of the obstacles ahead while caring enough about the outcome to keep reading. Most importantly, they should believe that this story could only happen to this specific character in this specific world – that the plot grows naturally from the elements you've established rather than feeling imposed from outside.

THE CHALLENGE OF ACT TWO

If Act One is about setting up possibilities, Act Two is about complicating them in interesting ways. Many stories struggle in maintaining tension through what can feel like a long middle section between the exciting beginning and climactic end. The key lies in understanding that Act Two isn't just about obstacles; it's about forcing your protagonist to grow and change through escalating challenges.

Think of Act Two as having two distinct halves, divided by what's often called the midpoint reversal. In the first half, your protagonist is typically reactive, responding to events and trying to find their footing in their new circumstances. The midpoint marks a crucial shift where they begin taking more active control of their situation, even if their actions don't always lead to success.

This structure works particularly well because it creates natural progression. Each sequence builds on what came before while raising the stakes. In *The Dresden Files*, for example, each case Harry Dresden tackles reveals new layers of supernatural politics and personal consequences, building toward major revelations that change how he sees his world. The early books might focus on relatively straightforward supernatural crimes, but each case exposes him to bigger players and deeper conspiracies.

I generally think about Act Two as happening in two parts, with a midpoint in the middle. The first half of Act Two should focus on three key elements:

First, your protagonist needs to learn the rules of their new reality. Whether they're entering a fantasy world, starting a new relationship, or taking on a dangerous investigation, they need to understand how things work in this new context. This learning process creates natural opportunities for both conflict and character development.

Second, they should face escalating challenges that test their existing skills and beliefs. These challenges should reveal both strengths and weaknesses, showing why they're the right person for this journey while highlighting what they still need to learn.

Third, they should begin forming relationships or alliances that will become important later. These connections might help them overcome immediate obstacles while setting up future complications or betrayals.

The midpoint reversal itself should do more than just surprise readers. It should fundamentally change the nature of the protagonist's challenge. This might mean revealing that what they thought was the problem is actually just a symptom of a deeper issue, discovering that someone they trusted has betrayed them, or realizing that achieving their goal will require sacrifices they hadn't anticipated.

Some effective approaches to midpoint reversals include:

- **The False Victory**: The protagonist achieves what they thought they wanted, only to discover it creates bigger problems or isn't what they really needed. Think of how in *The Hunger Games,* the rule change allowing two victors seems like salvation before becoming a source of deeper conflict.
- **The Game-Changing Revelation:** New information forces the protagonist to reevaluate everything they thought they knew. This works particularly well in mysteries and thrillers where discovering the true nature of the conspiracy changes how the protagonist must approach their investigation. It usually takes place at the end of Act 2.
- **The Raised Stakes:** The conflict expands beyond the protagonist's personal concerns to affect their community or world. This often marks the transition

from personal survival to heroic sacrifice, as the character must decide whether they're willing to risk everything for a larger cause.
- **The Return Home:** The protagonist returns to their ordinary world only to find it changed, or to realize they've changed too much to fit there anymore. This creates both external and internal conflict as they struggle with who they've become.

The second half of Act Two should show your protagonist becoming more proactive, making deliberate choices rather than just reacting to events. However, their early attempts at taking control should often fail or have unintended consequences. These failures force them to grow and adapt while maintaining tension through the middle of your story.

Some effective techniques for maintaining momentum through Act Two include:

Creating "nested tension" where multiple conflicts operate at different scales. While your protagonist deals with immediate challenges, larger threats should be developing in the background. This creates a sense of building pressure while providing variety in the types of conflicts they face.

Using set pieces, which are major scenes spaced roughly every 10,000 words that provide clear progression. These aren't just action sequences; they're pivotal moments that force character growth or revelation. Think of them as the tent poles that hold up your story's middle section.

Alternating between high-intensity sequences and quieter character moments that allow for emotional processing. These quieter moments aren't just about pacing – they're opportunities to deepen relationships, reveal character through conversation, and let readers process the implications of recent events.

Ensuring that each major revelation forces the protagonist to reevaluate their understanding or approach. New information shouldn't just advance the plot; it should challenge their assumptions and force them to adapt their strategies.

One common mistake in Act Two is introducing too many new elements rather than developing what's already established. While you can add complications, they should grow naturally from seeds planted in Act One. Think of it like juggling – you want to keep multiple plot threads in motion, but adding too many makes it impossible to maintain control.

Another crucial aspect is maintaining clear cause-and-effect relationships between events. Each scene should either result from previous events or set up future developments. Random obstacles might create temporary excitement but won't contribute to the story's overall momentum.

By the end of Act Two, your protagonist should be both more capable and more vulnerable than when they started – better equipped to face challenges but with more to lose. The stage should be set for Act Three's climactic confrontations while leaving readers genuinely uncertain about how things will resolve.

Frankly, Act Two is where most books fall apart. It has the fewest structural rules, which often leads bloated, meandering, confusing middles that frustrate readers. It often feels like writers are just padding books to hit their word count, but if you can use these points to keep your story moving forward, you should be able to avoid that fate

BUILDING TOWARD RESOLUTION

The final act of your story needs to do more than just resolve the plot. It also needs to deliver on the emotional promises you've made to readers throughout the story. This is where all the setup from Acts One and Two pays off in what should feel both surprising and inevitable. Creating this sense of inevitability while maintaining suspense requires careful attention to how you've developed both external and internal conflicts throughout your story.

Act Three typically comprises the final 25% of your story and involves several key elements that must work together harmoniously. The Crisis Point forces your protagonist to face their greatest challenge, usually through a choice that demonstrates how they've changed. The Climax brings the central conflict to its peak intensity, often mirroring earlier events but with crucial differences. The Resolution shows the aftermath and provides closure while maintaining energy.

Consider how *The Hunger Games* handles its final act. Katniss's ultimate crisis isn't just about physical survival – it's a moral choice about defying the Capitol that forces her to weigh individual survival against systemic change. This works because the story has carefully moved toward this moment through escalating challenges to her understanding of both the Games and her role within them.

The Crisis Point must force your protagonist to make a choice that:

- Connects directly to your story's central themes
- Challenges their core beliefs or deepest fears

- Demonstrates what they've learned through the story
- Has significant consequences for both success and failure
- Emerges naturally from previous events and character development

The Climax builds on this crisis to create peak intensity in both external and internal conflicts. Effective climaxes typically:

- Mirror elements from earlier in the story but with crucial differences showing growth
- Resolve both the external conflict and the protagonist's internal struggle
- Deliver emotional satisfaction while maintaining plausibility
- Demonstrate how characters have changed through their choices
- Create resonance with your story's themes through how conflicts are resolved

The Resolution then shows the aftermath of these events, providing closure while maintaining energy. This section should:

- Demonstrate how the story's events have changed both characters and their world
- Tie up significant plot threads while possibly leaving some questions open
- Provide emotional satisfaction without dragging on too long
- Reinforce your story's themes through how things end

- Create what Monica Leonelle calls "resonant closure", which are endings that feel complete while acknowledging life continues

One powerful technique for crafting an effective Act Three comes from "emotional escalation" ensuring that the stakes aren't just externally higher but emotionally more significant. The final challenge should force characters to confront their deepest fears or most closely held beliefs while demonstrating how they've grown through the story.

This often works best when Act Three mirrors elements from Act One, but with crucial differences that show character growth. The protagonist might return to their ordinary world but see it differently, face a similar challenge to one they failed at earlier but succeed through what they've learned, or confront their initial antagonist with new understanding developed through their journey.

Remember that resolution doesn't mean every question must be answered or every plot thread tied up neatly. What matters is providing satisfaction for the core emotional journey you've taken readers on while maintaining the energy that has driven your story forward. Minor plot elements can often be left to readers' imagination, while focusing on resolving the most significant relationships and changes.

The most common mistakes in Act Three usually involve either rushing to conclusion or dragging out the ending too long. The key is finding the right balance between providing satisfying closure and maintaining narrative momentum. This often means focusing on the most emotionally significant elements while letting minor threads resolve more quickly or remain slightly open.

Some crucial principles for crafting satisfying Act Threes:

- Ensure that the protagonist's success (or failure) comes from their own choices rather than external intervention or coincidence. They should earn their resolution through what they've learned and how they've changed. This maintains the story's internal logic while providing emotional satisfaction.
- Connect the climactic action to your story's thematic elements. The way characters resolve their conflicts should demonstrate or challenge the ideas you've been exploring throughout the story. This creates coherence between plot and theme.
- Show how the events of the story have changed not just the protagonist but their world and the people around them. This demonstrates the broader significance of the journey while providing closure on multiple levels.
- Monitor pacing carefully through the final act. While the climax might move quickly, both the crisis point and resolution often benefit from giving readers time to process the emotional weight of events. This creates what John Truby calls "emotional resonance" – the feeling that the ending matters on both plot and character levels.

ADVANCED PLOT DEVELOPMENT TECHNIQUES

While understanding basic plot structure is crucial, crafting truly engaging narratives requires mastering specific techniques for developing and maintaining story momentum. These advanced approaches help create the kind of narrative complexity that keeps readers invested while maintaining clear forward movement.

Russell Nohelty

The Levitz Paradigm provides a sophisticated approach to plot development. Instead of thinking of your story as a single thread, imagine juggling multiple plot lines at different stages of development:

- Your A-story drives the current scene or chapter
- B-stories develop in the background, ready to become future A-stories
- C-stories and D-stories are seeded for later development

This creates narrative density, the sense that your story world is rich with possibilities while maintaining clear focus on current events. *Game of Thrones* demonstrates this beautifully, with multiple character arcs developing simultaneously while each book maintains clear central conflicts.

Character-driven plotting ensures that major events emerge naturally from character choices rather than feeling imposed by the author. This involves:

- Understanding each character's core motivations and fears
- Creating situations that force difficult choices
- Ensuring that choices have meaningful consequences
- Building complications that arise from character decisions
- Maintaining consistency in how characters respond to challenges

Another powerful technique comes from having tensions operate at multiple levels simultaneously. While characters deal with immediate problems, larger threats loom in the background. This creates ongoing tension while providing various sources of conflict and resolution.

The "Two Standard Deviations Rule" offers guidance on introducing complexity gradually. No more than 10-20% of what you present should be completely unfamiliar to readers. This applies to both world-building and plot development, ensuring readers can follow increasingly complex storylines.

Some specific techniques for strengthening plot at every stage:

Early Development:

- Create character triangulation by showing protagonists in different contexts
- Plant seeds for future developments through seemingly minor details
- Establish clear stakes while hinting at deeper complications
- Build in thematic elements that can be developed throughout the story
- Create questions that drive reader curiosity

Middle Development:

- Use the Levitz Paradigm to juggle multiple plot threads
- Employ nested conflict to maintain tension at different scales
- Create meaningful reversals that change how characters understand their situation
- Develop subplots that illuminate main themes from different angles

- Build toward revelations that force character growth

Late Development:
- Bring plot threads together in surprising but logical ways
- Create resonance between early and late story elements
- Ensure resolutions emerge from character development
- Maintain tension while providing satisfying closure
- Leave room for reader interpretation where appropriate

Managing multiple plot threads requires understanding how different types of conflict interact. Consider having:

- Personal conflicts that drive character development
- Interpersonal conflicts that create immediate tension
- Larger conflicts that provide overarching structure
- Thematic conflicts that explore your story's central ideas

This layered approach helps maintain engagement while creating the kind of complexity that rewards careful reading. Each layer of conflict should illuminate different aspects of your characters and themes while contributing to the overall narrative.

Remember that even complex plots need clear focus. Use techniques like character-driven plotting and nested conflict to create richness without losing direction. Every plot element should serve your story's central themes and character development while maintaining forward momentum.

The goal isn't complexity for its own sake but creating the kind of narrative depth that keeps readers invested while delivering meaningful resolution. When these techniques work together effectively, they create stories that satisfy both emotional and intellectual levels while maintaining the forward momentum that keeps readers engaged until the final page.

Russell Nohelty

UNDERSTANDING THE RHYTHM OF STORY

Every story has a heartbeat. Like music, this pulse can quicken with excitement, slow for reflection, or build to a crescendo. Understanding how to control this rhythm, which we call pacing, is crucial for keeping readers engaged throughout your narrative. But pacing isn't just about fast versus slow; it's about creating a natural flow that serves your story's emotional and thematic needs.

Think about how a skilled musician uses tempo. A song doesn't maintain the same speed throughout. It builds, slows, creates tension, and releases it. The same principle applies to storytelling. *The Dresden Files* demonstrates this beautifully in how it structures its narratives. Jim Butcher begins each book with what he calls a "case of the week," establishing a rhythm that feels manageable and engaging. As the story progresses, he gradually increases complexity and stakes but always maintains a clear rhythm that keeps readers oriented.

This rhythm comes from understanding the fundamental unit of pacing: the scene-sequel structure. A scene is a unit of story where something happens. It has a goal, encounters conflict and ends in some form of disaster or complication. The sequel is the emotional aftermath, dealing with how characters react, what dilemmas they face, and what decisions they make. Together, these create the basic heartbeat of your story.

Consider how *Game of Thrones* uses this structure. When Ned Stark discovers the truth about Cersei's children, that's a scene. It has a clear goal (understanding why Jon Arryn died), conflict (the dangerous nature of the information), and disaster (the realization puts everyone he loves in danger). The sequel comes in how he processes this information, weighs his options, and ultimately decides to confront Cersei directly. This decision then leads to new scenes, creating a natural flow of action and reaction.

However, different genres require different rhythms. In thrillers, the sequels might be very short, with just enough to establish emotional stakes before moving to the next action sequence. In romance, sequels often run longer because the emotional processing is central to the story. The key is matching your pacing to your genre's expectations while maintaining enough variety to keep readers engaged.

One of the most common mistakes writers make is maintaining the same pace for too long. Even action scenes need moments of micro-tension and release. During a fight sequence, for instance, you might have quick exchanges of blows interspersed with brief moments where combatants assess each other or adjust their strategies. These variations create texture and prevent reader fatigue.

The opposite mistake is changing pace too frequently, never allowing readers to settle into a rhythm. Think of it like driving a car. The constant acceleration and braking makes for an uncomfortable ride. Instead, you want smooth transitions between different speeds, allowing each pace to establish itself before changing again.

Understanding pacing also means recognizing that it operates on multiple levels simultaneously. At the micro level, sentence and paragraph structure affect how quickly readers move through the text. Short, punchy sentences speed things up. Longer, more complex sentences slow things down and often signal more reflective moments. At the macro level, chapter structure and scene sequence create larger patterns of tension and release.

Consider how *The Expanse* handles these different levels. During space battles, the prose becomes terse and immediate, with short sentences and quick scene transitions creating a sense of urgency. During political discussions or character development scenes, the pace slows, allowing for more nuanced exploration of motivations and relationships. Yet these varying paces all serve the larger rhythm of each book's overall arc.

The most effective pacing often comes from understanding what we call "narrative promises." Every scene makes implicit promises to your readers about what kind of story they're reading and what kind of experience they can expect. Fast pacing promises excitement and quick resolution. Slower pacing promises deeper understanding or emotional revelation. Breaking these promises risks losing reader trust.

This brings us to one of the most crucial aspects of pacing: the relationship between tension and release. Every story needs both. Tension draws readers forward, making them want to know what happens next. Release gives them satisfaction and emotional payoff. The art lies in balancing these elements, creating what some writers call "the pleasurable uncertainty" that keeps readers engaged.

Think about how a television series like *The Mandalorian* handles this balance. Each episode typically contains its own tension-release cycle—a problem is presented, complications arise, and some form of resolution is achieved. But these individual cycles also contribute to larger season-long arcs, creating multiple layers of pacing that keep viewers invested across episodes.

Understanding these fundamentals of pacing provides the foundation for more sophisticated pacing techniques. As we move forward, we'll explore how to apply these principles practically, creating stories that keep readers engaged from the first page to the last.

THE MECHANICS OF MOMENTUM

Understanding how to control pacing begins with mastering what we call Motivation-Reaction Units, or the scene-sequel pattern. Every story moment can be broken down into these fundamental building blocks, and learning to manipulate them gives you precise control over your story's rhythm.

A scene consists of three essential elements: goal, conflict, and disaster. The goal is what your character wants to achieve. The conflict is what stands in their way. The disaster is how things go wrong, or sometimes, how they go right in an unexpected way that creates new complications. This structure creates forward momentum, pulling readers through your story with a sense of urgency and anticipation.

The sequel that follows is equally important, consisting of reaction, dilemma, and decision. This is where characters and readers process what just happened, consider options, and determine the next course of action. The length and depth of these elements determine how fast or slow your story feels at any given moment.

Consider how *The Hunger Games* uses this pattern. When Katniss volunteers for the reaping, that's a scene: her goal is to protect Prim, the conflict comes from the brutal reality of the Games, and the disaster is that she's now committed herself to potential death. The sequel shows her processing this choice during her goodbyes to family and friends, weighing her chances of survival, and finally deciding to promise Prim she'll try to win. This sequence works because both the scene and sequel receive the time they need—neither is rushed or prolonged beyond its natural length.

What many writers don't realize is that you can adjust pacing by manipulating the proportion between scenes and sequels. In fast-paced sections, sequels might just be a few sentences of reaction before moving to the next scene. In more emotionally driven moments, sequels might run longer than the scenes they follow, allowing readers to fully experience the emotional weight of what's happening.

The Dresden Files provides an excellent example of this flexibility. During action sequences, sequels might be as brief as Harry Dresden catching his breath and making a quick decision. During more character-focused moments, sequels expand to explore the moral and personal implications of his choices. This variation creates natural ebbs and flows in the story's pacing while maintaining forward momentum.

One of the most effective techniques for controlling pace is what we call "scene stacking." This involves planning key story moments, what film writers call "set pieces", approximately every 10,000 words. These major scenes serve as tent poles that hold up your narrative, creating a rhythm readers can subconsciously anticipate. The spaces between these set pieces allow for character development, world-building, and emotional processing.

The specific spacing of these moments often depends on your genre. Thrillers might stack major scenes closer together, while literary fiction might space them further apart. The key is maintaining enough forward momentum to keep readers engaged while giving them time to process significant events.

Take how *The Expanse* handles pacing in its space battles. The actual combat might only last a few minutes in story time, but the author can expand or contract these moments through scene and sequel manipulation. A crucial missile launch might get several pages of tense build-up, while the aftermath allows characters to process what happened and make decisions about their next moves.

Scene transitions also play a crucial role in pacing. Abrupt transitions create a sense of urgency and forward momentum. Smoother, more gradual transitions allow readers to settle into new scenes and process what's happened. Learning to vary your transitions gives you another tool for controlling story rhythm.

Recovery time between major events is crucial yet often overlooked. After significant scenes, readers need time to process what happened, but this doesn't mean the story has to slow to a crawl. Even quieter moments should move the story forward through character development, relationship evolution, or deepening understanding of the situation.

The *Game of Thrones* series handles this through its multiple viewpoint structure. After intense scenes, it often shifts to different characters in different locations, allowing readers to process major events while still maintaining engagement with the larger story. When it returns to the original plotline, readers have had time to absorb the impact of what happened.

Your scene structure can create nested tension. While each scene has its immediate goals and conflicts, it can simultaneously build toward larger story arcs. A conversation between characters might resolve an immediate conflict while seeding information that will become crucial later. This layering of purpose helps maintain momentum even in quieter moments.

In *Pride and Prejudice*, there is a crucial scene where Mr. Darcy, visibly restless and pacing in the same room as Elizabeth Bennet, finally breaks his silence to confess his love. This immediate, dramatic declaration is tension-packed in its own right, but it also unleashes deeper conflicts that hinge on social standing, pride, and misunderstanding.

Darcy's blunt approach heightens Elizabeth's wariness: his words solve the short-term mystery of whether he will speak, yet trigger new friction rooted in the distance between their social circles and personalities. Rather than tidy resolution, his confession ushers in a fresh wave of challenges ensuring that, beneath a momentary climax, currents of tension continue to drive the larger story forward.

One common pacing mistake is belief that constant action maintains tension. In reality, unrelenting action without proper sequels often reduces tension by exhausting readers and depriving them of the emotional context that makes action meaningful. Even the most fast-paced stories need variations in rhythm to maintain their impact.

Understanding these mechanical aspects of pacing allows you to create the sense that the story is always moving forward, even in its quieter moments. This comes from recognizing that pacing isn't about speed so much as it is about purpose. Every scene and sequel should serve the story's larger goals while maintaining its own internal rhythm.

The key to mastering these mechanics lies in practice and awareness. Start by analyzing books in your genre, noting how they handle the balance between scenes and sequels. Pay attention to how they stack major moments and handle recovery time. Then experiment with these techniques in your own writing, always remembering that the goal is to serve your story's emotional and thematic needs rather than adhering to rigid rules.

THE EMOTIONAL ENGINE OF PACING

The most powerful pacing doesn't come from mechanical structure alone but emerges from the emotional journey of your characters. Understanding how to align your story's rhythm with its emotional beats creates the story's speed and makes the flow feel natural because they match the emotional experience of both characters and readers.

In the intro to this book, we talked about how Taylor Swift structures her albums. In "Tortured Poets Department," she doesn't just arrange songs randomly. She creates an emotional journey where each piece builds on what came before. Fast, angry songs provide release for tension built up in slower, more reflective pieces. This same principle applies to written stories. The pace of your narrative should mirror and support the emotional experience you're trying to create.

This emotional pacing begins with understanding your characters' core wounds and desires. When characters face situations that trigger these fundamental aspects of their psychology, the pacing naturally slows to allow readers to fully experience these moments. *The Hunger Games* demonstrates this beautifully in how it handles Katniss's protective instincts toward Prim and later Rue. The story slows down during these moments not because of arbitrary structure but because these interactions touch the emotional core of who Katniss is.

Different emotional states demand different pacing approaches. Anger and fear often benefit from faster pacing that mirrors the quickened pulse and shortened attention span of these emotions. Grief and love often require slower pacing, giving readers time to process complex feelings alongside the characters. The key is to match your story's rhythm to the emotional experience you want readers to have.

This becomes particularly crucial during character transformations. Major changes in how characters see themselves or their world need time to feel earned. The pacing should reflect the difficulty and significance of these changes. When characters face their core wounds or challenge their fundamental beliefs, rushing through these moments robs them of their impact.

Consider how *The Crown* handles these transformational moments. When Elizabeth must choose between her sister's happiness and her duty as monarch, the show slows its pace considerably. We spend time with her as she wrestles with this decision, understanding its personal and historical weight. The slower pace makes her eventual choice feel both inevitable and devastating precisely because we've experienced the full emotional journey that led to it.

Emotional pacing also involves moments when current events echo or contrast with earlier experiences. When characters face situations that mirror previous challenges, slightly slowing the pace allows readers to make these connections and appreciate how the character has grown or changed. These moments create emotional depth without explicitly stating the comparison.

The *Game of Thrones* series masters this technique through its parallel character arcs. When different characters face similar moral choices in different contexts, the pacing slows just enough to let readers draw the connections. This creates thematic resonance while maintaining narrative momentum.

One of the most powerful tools for emotional pacing is the "quiet before the storm." These are moments of relative calm that allow tension to build while giving readers time to understand the emotional stakes of what's coming. They work not because they're structurally necessary but because they mirror how humans actually experience anticipation and dread.

This principle extends to how we handle aftermath scenes. After major emotional events, characters and readers need time to process what happened. This doesn't mean the story stops moving. Instead, the pace shifts to accommodate reflection while maintaining forward momentum through smaller conflicts or relationship developments.

Character relationships also influence pacing naturally. Scenes between characters with established relationships often move more quickly because they can communicate more with less. Scenes between characters still building trust or understanding might need more time to develop nuance and subtext. This variation creates natural rhythm while serving character development.

Consider how romantic relationships develop in well-paced stories. Initial attraction might be conveyed through quick, energetic scenes, but as the relationship deepens, the pacing often slows to explore more complex emotional territory. This isn't just about following genre conventions—it's about matching the natural rhythm of how relationships develop.

One of the most common mistakes in emotional pacing is rushing through important character moments to get to the next plot point. This often happens when writers focus too much on external pacing (what's happening in the plot) and not enough on internal pacing (how characters are processing and changing through events).

The key to avoiding this lies in understanding that emotional impact often comes from contrast. A character making a quick decision can be powerful precisely because we've seen them agonize over choices before. A fast-paced action sequence hits harder when it's bracketed by moments of emotional significance that give it context and meaning.

This brings us to what might be the most crucial aspect of emotional pacing: authenticity. The rhythm of your story should feel true to how humans actually experience and process emotions. This doesn't mean slavishly copying real-time emotional processing, of course. Stories necessarily compress and heighten experience. But the emotional journey should feel genuine, with pacing that supports rather than undermines this authenticity.

GENRE-SPECIFIC PACING STRATEGIES

Every genre has its own unique rhythm that serves its particular storytelling needs while fulfilling readers' expectations. Understanding these patterns helps you create stories that feel both fresh and familiar, innovating within established frameworks that readers understand intuitively.

Romance novels, for example, require a specific pacing approach that balances external and internal conflicts. The genre's focus on emotional development means sequels often run longer than in other types of fiction. When characters process their feelings, make difficult choices about relationships, or confront their fears about intimacy, the pacing naturally slows to give these moments the weight they deserve. Consider how romance authors handle the aftermath of a breakup scene. The actual break might be relatively quick, but the emotional processing afterward often extends across several scenes or even chapters.

This doesn't mean romance can't move quickly when needed. The "meet cute" that opens almost every romance novel often employs faster pacing to create energy and immediate reader engagement. The key lies in understanding when to speed up and when to slow down based on the emotional weight of the moment. Lucy Score's *Knockemout* series demonstrates this by using quick, humorous exchanges to establish character dynamics while slowing down for deeper emotional revelations that drive the central romance.

Thrillers and suspense novels present a different challenge. These genres typically maintain higher baseline tension, but even here, constant high-speed pacing can exhaust readers. The solution lies in varying the rhythm within scenes while maintaining overall momentum. During a chase sequence, for instance, you might have bursts of intense action interspersed with brief moments where characters must hide or strategize, creating natural ebbs and flows within the larger fast-paced framework.

The Dresden Files, while technically urban fantasy, often employs thriller-style pacing in its action sequences. Harry Dresden's investigations might move at a measured pace, but when supernatural conflict erupts, the pacing quickens dramatically. However, even in these faster sequences, author Jim Butcher includes brief moments of reflection or strategy that prevent reader fatigue while maintaining tension.

Fantasy and science fiction face unique pacing challenges because of their world-building requirements. These genres must balance the need to explain new concepts and settings with maintaining narrative momentum. The most successful approaches often integrate world-building naturally into character actions and conflicts rather than stopping the story for exposition. *The Expanse* handles this masterfully by revealing its complex solar system politics through character conflicts and decisions rather than information dumps.

Mystery novels require perhaps the most careful pacing of all. These stories must maintain reader engagement while parceling out information at precisely the right rate—too fast and the solution feels unearned, too slow and readers lose interest. Successful mystery writers often use what we call "layered pacing," where multiple storylines move at different speeds. A primary investigation might move steadily forward while subplots provide variety in pacing and emotional texture.

This layered approach works in other genres as well. *Game of Thrones* uses multiple viewpoint characters not just to tell a broader story, but to create pacing variety. While one storyline might be reaching a dramatic climax, another might be in a quieter phase of development, allowing readers to experience different emotional rhythms while maintaining overall engagement.

Literary fiction often employs a rhythm that matches the mental and emotional states of its characters. In these works, external action might be minimal, but the internal rate at which revelations occur and understanding deepens creates momentum. This approach requires careful attention to how readers process information and emotion, ensuring each realization has space to land while maintaining forward movement.

Regardless of genre, one universal principle remains: the pacing must serve the story. While different genres have different conventions, these aren't rigid rules but rather frameworks that help readers engage with your particular type of story. Understanding these frameworks allows you to work within them effectively while finding opportunities for innovation.

Russell Nohelty

You can also take the pacing from one genre and map it onto another. My series, *The Godsverse Chronicles*, is a fantasy novel with the pacing of an action-adventure novel.

The key lies in recognizing the implicit agreements you make with readers based on your genre choice. A thriller promises regular doses of tension and excitement. A romance promises emotional depth and relationship development. A mystery promises gradual revelation leading to satisfying resolution. Breaking these promises, or fulfilling them in ways that feel awkward, risks losing reader engagement.

Consider how cross-genre works handle these different pacing needs. A romantic subplot in a thriller needs to find moments for emotional development without destroying the main story's tension. A mystery element in a fantasy novel must balance investigation pacing with world-building needs. Success comes from understanding how different pacing approaches can work together rather than conflict.

The most sophisticated writing often comes from understanding these genre expectations well enough to play with them intentionally. You might slow the pace at a moment when genre conventions suggest speeding up, but if this choice serves a clear purpose and you've built reader trust, it can create powerful effects. The key is to ensure these variations feel purposeful rather than arbitrary.

Remember that genre conventions exist because they work. They've evolved to serve particular types of stories effectively. Learning to work within these conventions while maintaining your unique voice and vision is part of mastering the craft of storytelling. Your goal isn't to ignore genre expectations but to understand them well enough to fulfill them in fresh, engaging ways.

ADVANCED PACING TECHNIQUES AND PROBLEM-SOLVING

Mastering pacing ultimately comes down to understanding how to diagnose and solve rhythm problems in your story. Even experienced writers sometimes find their stories dragging in places or moving too quickly in others. The key lies in recognizing these issues early and knowing how to adjust your story's rhythm without losing its essential energy.

One of the most powerful advanced pacing techniques involves what we call "nested tension." This approach creates multiple layers of pacing operating simultaneously. Think about how *The Expanse* handles its major plot developments. While immediate conflicts drive scene-level tension, larger political machinations create series-level tension, and character relationships provide emotional tension. These different layers operate at different speeds, creating a rich, engaging reading experience.

This layered approach proves particularly effective in series writing. *The Dresden Files* demonstrates this through its careful balance of immediate case-related tension and longer-term character and world development. Each book must maintain its own satisfying pace while contributing to larger series arcs. Jim Butcher achieves this by ensuring each book has what he calls set pieces, which are major scenes spaced roughly every ten thousand words, while seeding elements that will become important in future books.

Understanding how to diagnose pacing problems starts with recognizing common symptoms. A story moving too quickly often jumps from event to event without giving readers time to process their emotional impact. This frequently happens when writers worry about maintaining tension at the expense of emotional depth. The solution isn't necessarily to slow everything down, but rather to identify key emotional moments that deserve more space and attention.

Conversely, stories that move too slowly often suffer from so much time on character reflection and emotional processing that the narrative momentum stalls. This doesn't mean emotional depth is wrong. It means you need to find ways to maintain forward movement even during introspective moments. *The Crown* achieves this by having characters process emotions while still dealing with immediate political or personal challenges, creating what we call "active reflection."

Another advanced technique involves pacing moments that deliberately mirror earlier story rhythms to create thematic resonance. *Game of Thrones* uses this effectively when characters face similar moral choices in different contexts. The pacing of these echo moments often mirrors the original scene's rhythm, creating subconscious connections for readers while maintaining story momentum.

Recovery time between major events presents another common pacing challenge. Many writers struggle with finding the right balance between giving readers time to process significant events and maintaining engagement. The solution often lies in scenes that allow emotional processing while still moving the story forward through character development, relationship evolution, or subplot advancement.

This brings us to one of the most sophisticated pacing techniques, which is using rhythm changes to create meaning. When you establish a consistent pace and then deliberately break it, that change itself becomes meaningful. Consider how romance novels often speed up the pacing just before a major relationship revelation, then slow dramatically for the emotional aftermath. This rhythm change helps readers feel the impact of the moment more deeply.

Flashbacks and time jumps present their own pacing challenges. The key lies in understanding that these devices shouldn't just provide background information. They should create their own tension while illuminating present events. Successful flashbacks often maintain a different but equally engaging pace from the main narrative, creating what we call "temporal counterpoint."

One particularly challenging aspect of pacing involves handling large cast stories. Different character arcs naturally move at different speeds, which can create pacing inconsistencies if not handled carefully. The solution often involves deliberately alternating between different character arcs based on their emotional and narrative intensity. This creates natural variations in pace while maintaining overall story momentum.

Information revelation, particularly in mysteries or stories with complex plots, requires especially careful pacing consideration. The key lies in understanding the difference between "information pacing" and "action pacing." Information can be revealed slowly even during fast-paced sequences, or quickly during slower, more reflective moments. The crucial factor is ensuring the rate of revelation maintains reader engagement without creating confusion.

Series pacing presents perhaps the most complex challenge of all. Each book must satisfy as an individual story while contributing to larger series arcs. This requires understanding what we call "nested satisfaction", which is how to create complete emotional and narrative arcs within each book while maintaining tension that carries readers to the next installment.

When troubleshooting pacing problems, start by mapping your story's emotional and tension arcs. Look for places where the pacing doesn't match the emotional weight of what's happening. Pay particular attention to transition points where the rhythm changes. These changes should feel natural rather than jarring, serving clear narrative purposes rather than happening arbitrarily.

Pacing isn't just about speed. It's about rhythm, tension, and release. Even fast-paced stories need variation in their rhythm to maintain impact. Even slow-paced stories need enough forward momentum to keep readers engaged. The goal isn't to maintain any particular pace but to create a rhythm that serves your story's emotional and narrative needs while keeping readers invested in what happens next.

The most sophisticated pacing often comes from understanding these principles well enough to break them intentionally for effect. But such violations of expected rhythm only work when they serve clear narrative purposes and when you've built enough reader trust through consistently strong pacing in other areas. Master the rules first. Then, you can break them in ways that make your story stronger rather than weaker.

STORY COHESION

At the heart of every memorable story lies a central force that binds all elements together into a cohesive whole. Think of this force as the gravitational center of your narrative universe. Every character, plot point, and world detail orbits around it, held in perfect balance by its pull. This might be a theme, a character journey, or a central question, but whatever form it takes, it must be strong enough to unify every aspect of your story.

Understanding this center is crucial because it guides every decision you make as a writer. Consider how *The Hunger Games* builds its entire narrative around themes of survival and systemic oppression. These aren't just intellectual concepts floating above the story. They're woven into its very fabric.

The contrast between Capitol excess and district deprivation isn't merely world-building; it's a physical manifestation of the theme. Character relationships explore different approaches to survival, from Katniss's protective instincts to Haymitch's cynical adaptation to Peeta's emphasis on maintaining humanity at all costs. Even the games themselves, with their emphasis on entertainment and spectacle, reinforce how power maintains control through manipulation of basic human needs.

This foundation creates what we call "thematic resonance", which is the way different story elements echo and reinforce each other. In *Game of Thrones*, the harsh realities of the world shape character personalities, which in turn influence plot decisions, which then affect the world itself. When Ned Stark's rigid honor meets the political intrigues of King's Landing, the resulting conflict feels inevitable precisely because every element, from the world's established rules to Ned's consistent characterization, works together to create that moment.

However, this doesn't mean every element must mirror the others. Sometimes the strongest cohesion comes through intentional contrast. When Katniss's small acts of compassion stand out against the games' brutality, both elements become more powerful through their juxtaposition. The key is that every element, whether through harmony or contrast, serves the story's central purpose.

Finding your story's center often begins with asking yourself fundamental questions: What truth are you trying to explore? What question are you trying to answer? What aspect of the human experience are you trying to illuminate? The answers to these questions become the foundation upon which you build everything else.

Consider how *The Expanse* uses questions about human nature and civilization as its center. Every plot development, character arc, and world-building detail explores how humans adapt, cooperate, and conflict as they spread through the solar system. The political tensions between Earth, Mars, and the Belt aren't just background. They're central to understanding how the environment shapes society and human development. Character conflicts arise naturally from these fundamental tensions, creating a story where personal and systemic issues intertwine seamlessly.

Your center also helps determine what belongs in your story and what doesn't. If an element doesn't somehow connect to or illuminate your central theme or question, it probably doesn't belong, no matter how interesting it might be on its own. This doesn't mean every element must obviously connect to your theme, especially since subtle connections often work better than obvious ones, but the connection should be there.

The best way to test if you've found a strong center is to examine how it connects to different story elements. Can you trace how it influences your world-building choices? Does it help explain character motivations and conflicts? Does it give weight to your plot developments? If you can't find these connections, you might need to either strengthen your center or choose a different one that better serves your story.

You'll know you've found the right center when it starts generating story possibilities naturally. A strong center doesn't just unite existing elements. It suggests new ones. When you understand that *The Hunger Games* is fundamentally about survival and systemic oppression, new character dynamics and plot developments suggest themselves. What happens when characters have different definitions of survival? How do various forms of oppression intersect and reinforce each other? These questions generate story possibilities while maintaining cohesion because they all connect to the central theme.

Remember that your story's center can evolve as you write, but this evolution should feel natural rather than arbitrary. The questions you're exploring might become more complex or nuanced, but they should remain recognizably connected to your original foundation. Think of how *The Hunger Games* expands from personal survival to questioning the nature of revolution and social change. It's a natural progression that builds on established themes rather than abandoning them.

Understanding your story's center isn't just about creating cohesion. It's about giving your story purpose and power. When every element works together to explore a central truth or question, your story becomes more than the sum of its parts. It becomes an experience that stays with readers long after they've finished the last page, because everything they encountered served a larger purpose than just entertainment.

BUILDING INTERCONNECTED ELEMENTS

Once you've established your story's gravitational center, it's time to figure out how everything else, characters, conflicts, subplots, world details—spirals around it. A book or series that "fires on all cylinders" typically features elements that don't just coexist but *speak* to each other, forming a web of relationships. Each aspect of the story, no matter how small, resonates with or contrasts the others, and in doing so, illuminates the core.

One of the most effective techniques for uniting story elements is to deliberately create **echoes**, which are moments or images in different chapters or books that mirror each other. Sometimes these echoes take the form of repeated phrases or images that shift slightly each time they appear. A romance heroine in Book One might vow she can "fix him" only to realize "I can't fix him" in Book Three. A single phrase repeated with a twist can jolt readers into seeing how a character's worldview has changed. In my books, characters often say, "You always have a choice. It just might not be a good one." Depending on who is talking, it hits different every time.

Parallels function similarly. You might place two characters on parallel journeys, each struggling with the same thematic question from opposing angles. In a series like *The Crown*, Elizabeth and Margaret reflect two ways of grappling with the monarchy's constraints—one stoic, one rebellious. Their parallel arcs create a sense of a unified canvas, even as each sister's choices lead to drastically different outcomes.

Contrasts, meanwhile, can sharpen your theme by pushing elements to opposite extremes. Think of the Capitol's flamboyant fashion contrasted against District 12's gray poverty in *The Hunger Games*. The disparity reinforces the story's message about systemic injustice, making each environment appear even more vivid and symbolically charged.

Cohesion deepens when **subplots** reinforce the central theme instead of drifting off on tangents. A detective might be solving a murder case (main plot) while grappling with guilt over a personal betrayal (subplot). Both revolve around the theme of trust and deception, linking the external conflict (tracking down a killer) and the internal conflict (atoning for mistakes).

Characters are often the greatest catalyst for interconnections because human relationships naturally mirror or clash with one another's beliefs. When two characters hold polarized views on the same thematic issue, the friction between them generates subplots that feel integral rather than add-ons. Taylor Swift's *Tortured Poets Department* features songs that focus on heartbreak from various angles: the partner who left, the narrator's own regrets, the possibility of loving someone new in the midst of old wounds. Each track (like each subplot) stands alone yet collectively forms a tapestry of heartbreak and self-discovery.

Recurrence fosters unity. Maybe you keep returning to a single color (blue for heartbreak, red for betrayal), a symbolic object (wedding rings, broken lockets), or a phrase that changes meaning each time it surfaces. Motifs act like a secret handshake with attentive readers: they recognize these reappearances and feel rewarded by how you evolve them.

In a comedic novel, you might introduce a running joke, like a minor character's obsession with conspiracies, that later becomes the key to unveiling the true conspiracy in the final act. Because the joke was there all along, its payoff feels deserved. A cameo, a snippet of dialogue, or a fleeting reference can all unify the reading experience, making the audience delight in how you weave each piece into the story's tapestry.

For writers building a connected universe or simply forging a consistent "brand," **echoing your older stories** can be immensely satisfying. Taylor Swift famously references her earlier songs in new albums, adopting a phrase or chord progression only to twist it. Authors who have published multiple series sometimes drop cameos or small Easter eggs that hint at a shared world. This practice not only unites your works thematically but also rewards loyal readers who pick up on those connections. Each subtle link invites readers deeper into your creative ecosystem.

Yet you have to strike a balance. Too many self-referential nods can alienate new fans if they feel excluded from an "in-group." The best references either stand fine on their own or provide enough context that new readers won't feel lost. Think of it as inviting them to share in the insider wink rather than shutting them out.

In the end, the process of building interconnected elements asks you to remain mindful of how each aspect of your story can reinforce others—like instruments in a band. When they play in harmony or in dynamic counterpoint, the cumulative experience is richer, more intense, and more memorable.

MANAGING GROWTH AND CHANGE

There often comes a moment in a writer's journey where the story starts to expand in ways you didn't anticipate. Perhaps your standalone novel spawns a sequel, then another. A cozy setting or fantastical world grows more complex with each new subplot or spin-off. Readers clamor for side characters to get their own arcs. Before you know it, you're standing before an ever-broadening tapestry of cast and conflicts.

Growth in a story or series can be wondrous and fantastical, or a Taylor Swift album that begins with a heartbreak concept and organically adds layers of reflection, brand-new vantage points, and behind-the-scenes "vault" tracks.

Yet you have to guard against expansions that feel haphazard. A new element or subplot should still revolve around your central theme; otherwise, the narrative can splinter under its own weight.

In short, each addition should answer a critical question: *Does this new element serve the story's core in some meaningful way?* If you can't identify how it illuminates or complicates your central theme, it may end up diluting your story instead of enhancing it.

Think of your story's environment as a house. Sometimes, instead of adding a brand-new wing, you need to **remodel** a room you already have. Adding dimension to a subculture, group dynamic, or ongoing character arc often creates stronger attachment for readers than introducing a half-dozen new realms or sidekicks. *The Mandalorian* exemplifies this concept. Rather than endlessly escalating cosmic threats, it deepens existing relationships and cultural nuances (Mandalorian beliefs, the foundling tradition) to keep the story grounded and emotionally resonant.

Expansion often works best when it's **incremental**. A side character from Book One might reveal a hidden motivation in Book Two, giving the reader a fresh window into your world. Maybe that once-minor figure is the star of Book Three. Each "bloom" of the story feels justified because it emerged naturally from seeds planted early on.

Stagnation can be as problematic as runaway escalation. If you never evolve your characters or world, the narrative becomes repetitive. If you escalate so dramatically that you're forever chasing bigger explosions or higher body counts, your story eventually hits a ceiling (or breaks continuity). The trick is to watch for organic pivot points. A character who spent three books defending their home might finally decide to venture beyond it. A monarchy that's been stable for centuries can face a quiet but corrosive threat that changes its entire identity.

Sometimes you realize that your once-cohesive series no longer excites you or your readers. That's a cue to either **pivot in a new direction** (giving a formerly passive character center stage) or wrap the storyline. Think of how certain authors conclude a beloved series so it remains a complete, fulfilling entity, rather than dragging it out for diminishing returns. Or how Taylor Swift, rather than endlessly repeating her earlier country aesthetic, shifted to pop, then folk, preserving her essential emotional core while refreshing the presentation.

Overextension often happens when authors feel pressured to outdo their last installment by ramping up the stakes beyond reason. The result can be a jarring shift that betrays the promise of earlier books. *The Vampire Diaries*, for example, wrote itself into a corner by introducing successively more powerful foes and apocalyptic threats, forcing a partial reset just to keep the story credible.

Rather than fixating on bigger external stakes, ask how your expansions deepen the **internal** stakes. How do new challenges test your character's evolving beliefs? How does the expansion cast your core theme in a more nuanced light? The real currency of a story is never how many cities you blow up; it's how deeply you let readers into the hearts and dilemmas of the characters who must navigate each blow.

LAYERING INFORMATION AND REVELATION

Cohesion thrives on **when** and **how** you reveal the essential truths of your story. A well-timed reveal can electrify readers, whereas dumping all the information at once can overwhelm or kill suspense. Think of your story as an unfolding puzzle. Your center is the picture on the box, but you choose how the pieces slot into place, one scene at a time.

Revelation works best in **tiers**. A detail in Chapter 3 might create curiosity but no immediate payoff. Only in Chapter 8 do readers see how it ties back to a side character's hidden agenda. By letting the audience connect the dots rather than spoon-feeding them from page one, you keep them engaged. This principle applies equally to thriller reveals and to relationship arcs in romance. A small gesture or passing comment might explode with significance in the final act, recontextualizing everything before.

You want the reader to stay grounded in the familiar while you slip in the new, whether that new is a fantasy magic system or a hidden emotional wound in your protagonist.

A hallmark of great layering is repetition with variation. Taylor Swift often takes a familiar phrase ("love of my life") and twists it at the last second ("loss of my life"), forcing listeners to reinterpret the entire narrative of that song. In novels, an incantation or repeated vow might morph slightly each time it appears, signaling your protagonist's changing mindset or the world's evolving rules.

When you echo a line or object introduced in Book One deep into Book Four, it should not feel random. Let the context shift so that the same phrase carries new emotional weight just as the behind-the-scenes tracks on a re-recorded album might reveal hidden heartbreak that redefines an earlier hit. Layered repetition grants your story a sense of inevitability and depth, because the seeds were there all along.

Sometimes you want to hold back a critical piece of information until the right moment. This approach helps you build tension and puzzle-box intrigue. However, the withheld detail must integrate seamlessly once revealed. If the big twist feels gratuitous, like something you dropped in purely for shock value, it will fracture cohesion rather than enhance it. **Everything** that follows the reveal (or precedes it) should confirm that this puzzle piece was missing, but the space for it existed all along.

Your supporting cast plays a large role here. They can embody partial truths, half-secrets, or contradictory beliefs that hint at the revelation to come. In *Game of Thrones*, cryptic references to the White Walkers pepper the early seasons, overshadowed by more immediate political drama, so that when the undead threat finally surges, it doesn't come out of nowhere.

While layering details about your world or plot, remember that layering emotional or thematic truths can prove equally compelling. A character's outward bravado might crumble in a series of small cracks, offhand remarks, unusual alliances, or nights of sleepless guilt. Each layering eventually converges in a confessional moment or a pivotal choice that resonates with your story's center.

Layered revelations aren't just about the final gotcha. They're also about watching your characters navigate partial knowledge, argue or bond over incomplete understandings, and ultimately see the deeper reality beneath the illusions. It's the emotional charge of discovery, of, "Oh, that's what was really going on," that sticks in the reader's mind.

MAINTAINING COHESION OVER TIME

A single novel is challenging enough, but maintaining cohesion across multiple books, expansions, or re-releases can feel like orchestrating an entire symphony. Here's where the longevity of authors like Terry Pratchett or the evolution of a multi-era phenomenon like *Taylor's Version* come into play. How do you keep your core themes and emotional promises intact, even as your cast, subplots, or media formats grow?

First, recognize that your story can grow in many ways, like new characters, new spinoff series, or alternate points of view, but one essential *emotional truth* should persist. *Discworld* morphs from comedic sketches to pointed social satire to heartfelt explorations of morality, yet the series always retains Pratchett's signature comedic voice and philosophical bent. Even when you drift into comedic side plots or epic tragedies, remember the gravitational center that started it all.

Long-running series often reward readers through subtle echoes that span multiple installments. A minor comment in Book One might become the central conflict in Book Six. Or a question teased in a short story suddenly finds an answer in a late-series novel. Good foreshadowing is everything for a series.

These callbacks form an emotional and intellectual tapestry that gives longtime fans a sense of belonging. They become insiders who spot the pattern. *The Crown* does this over different historical periods, letting each new season echo earlier arcs about duty, identity, and personal cost. Because the themes endure even when the cast changes, viewers feel the series is one coherent piece.

One of the trickiest aspects of a long-term saga is balancing the need to stay fresh with the obligation not to contradict or trivialize earlier canon. This challenge mirrors Taylor Swift's re-recording of her albums. How do you add behind-the-scenes songs from "the vault" without destroying the carefully crafted arc of the original release? You give context. You remain faithful to the original emotional journey but find artful ways to expand or refine it.

In writing, this might manifest as gentle recaps woven into later books, ensuring new readers can jump in. Or standalones set in the same world that reference crucial events but frame them from a new vantage point, so longtime fans see familiar arcs from fresh angles. You want to invite new fans without overshadowing the earlier books that built your world's reputation in the first place.

No matter how much success you've had, if you feel yourself burning out on a beloved world or theme, it's okay to pivot. Often, the best approach is to do so in a way that still respects the existing structure. Maybe you shift genres but bring over a side character or a shared mythos to unify it with your previous work. Or you adopt a radical new tone while preserving that core question. Just as Taylor Swift moved from country ballads to pop anthems to introspective folk, you can evolve your style without losing your central creative obsessions, those seeds that drew readers in from the start.

THE EVOLUTION OF A CREATIVE CAREER

Writers who've been at it for a decade or more often discover they've circled back to the same few emotional truths, retelling them in fresh contexts. This is not laziness. It's the hallmark of a coherent author brand. You might recast your "princess problems" in a futuristic intergalactic empire or retell your "found family" trope in a small-town drama. Each iteration becomes another piece of an ever-larger mosaic. Far from alienating your fans, these echoes unify your oeuvre, reinforcing your creative fingerprint.

In the end, cohesion over time isn't about repeating yourself. It's about **continuity with evolution** and holding on to your gravitational center while letting characters and conflicts grow more complex, letting revelations deepen or subvert what came before, and welcoming new audiences without discarding the loyal readers who fell in love with your world's earliest iterations.

A cohesive story, be it a single novel, a multi-volume epic, or an album that weaves heartbreak into every chord, begins with a defined center. That center might be an unanswerable question about human nature, a single theme you can't stop revisiting, or a particular emotional truth that drew you to writing in the first place. Around that nucleus, you layer interconnected elements that echo or contrast one another, you expand naturally without sacrificing your message, you reveal information at just the right pace, and you remain mindful of how every subplot, character, or callback reinforces the whole.

Russell Nohelty

It's a dance between **foundation** and **discovery**, between **the established core** and **the evolving frontier** of your creativity. The best stories feel coherent yet surprising, familiar yet inventive. They give the reader that sense of stepping into a rich tapestry, where every thread eventually converges on a single design. Whether your medium is a 400-page novel or a concept album, the principle is the same: a strong center, carefully woven connections, and a willingness to let the story grow in the directions that matter most.

If you've ever listened to an album that flows seamlessly from the first track to the last, or a series that completes its final book with an echo of the very first page, you know that unique sense of satisfaction, even awe. As an author, you can deliver that same experience. All it takes is the discipline to keep your focus, the courage to expand, the patience to reveal truths gradually, and the determination to maintain cohesion even when your story evolves in unexpected ways.

So long as you remain loyal to the gravitational center you've chosen—and let every new element, every twist, every reveal circle back to it—your story can continue, confidently and cohesively, as far as your imagination and your readers' devotion will carry it.

CRAFTING A PUBLISHABLE BOOK

I could have ended this book with the last chapter, but I wanted to quickly touch on how to take this book and bring it over the finish line into something you can publish with pride, which means taking some time to talk about editing and packaging.

Think of editing not as a single pass through your manuscript, but as a series of increasingly focused layers, starting with what many writers call a "garbage draft" or "zero draft." **This initial transfer from outline to prose isn't really editing at all.** It's about getting the raw material of your story onto the page. The term "garbage draft" is intentionally self-deprecating because it frees you from the paralysis of perfectionism. When you acknowledge upfront that this version will be rough, you give yourself permission to simply create.

Once you have your garbage draft completed, you can begin the actual editing process, which typically involves three distinct passes, each with its own focus:

The first draft focuses on major structural issues. This is where you're looking for the big problems: characters whose personalities shift inexplicably between the beginning and end of the story, plot threads that appear or disappear without resolution, or major inconsistencies in your world-building.

Think of this as examining your story's skeleton - you're making sure all the major bones are in place and properly connected before worrying about the smaller details.

The second draft moves to a more granular level. By this point, your word count should be relatively stable (around 95% of your final target), and your chapters should be in their final positions. This is where you begin "prettying up" the prose, ensuring each scene flows naturally into the next and that your pacing feels right. You're now looking at your story's musculature and how all the pieces work together to create smooth movement.

The third draft is about refinement and polish. You're now operating at the sentence level, looking for awkward phrasings, repetitive word choices, and opportunities to strengthen your prose. However - and this is crucial - you need to recognize when you've hit the point of diminishing returns.

If you find yourself making only marginal improvements rather than significant ones, it's time to hand your manuscript over to professional editors.

If you have trouble knowing when to pass off your story, you're in good company. ***Many writers stumble knowing when to let go.*** A useful guideline is to watch for the transition from exponential to marginal improvements. When you find yourself spending increasing time making smaller and smaller changes, that's your signal to seek outside expertise.

To make this process manageable, consider using **the Pomodoro Technique**, focused 25-minute work sessions followed by short breaks. When you're just starting out, aim for achievable goals like editing 250 words in a session. Over time, as your editing skills improve, you can gradually increase your pace. Many writers find they can eventually edit 4,000-5,000 words per hour during their first-draft structural edit, though it's important to note this speed comes with experience. There are also all sorts of groups and apps that can help make this more fun than maddening.

Remember that editing is ultimately about serving your story and your readers. The goal isn't to catch every possible error - that's what proofreaders are for. Instead, focus on this essential question: "Does anything here break the illusion of the story?" If something pulls readers out of the narrative, that's what needs your attention. Everything else is secondary.

FINDING A GREAT EDITOR

One of the reasons that people hate editing is because you can literally edit forever. I have never seen a draft of my books, even once they are published, that couldn't use more editing. The best skill you can have in writing is knowing when your book is done. It's a combination of skill and intuition, and I'll try to break it down for you.

Every author has their own cutoff point before their book goes to the editor, and the important thing is to have a system. Any successful writer has a system which works for them, and it evolves over the years, but without a system you'll never stop editing. Unfortunately, writing the draft is the easy part.

I'm going to share with you my process, but first I want to talk about the three types of editors you should have in your corner.

- **Developmental editor:** This is the editor every author should find at the beginning of their career, before they know structure or character creation or editing. These are the most expensive editors to hire, but they will be with you from the outline stage and help make sure your story makes sense. They will guide you through the whole process. They can spend days or weeks with you, hammering out your drafts and making sure they work cohesively. Not every writer needs a developmental editor, and you will probably grow out of the need for one over time, but if you've never written anything long form before, or if you've written in other formats than a novel, it's important to find this editor. They'll tell you if you're wasting your time, and how to improve more quickly than you can do yourself. At the beginning of your career your skills are underdeveloped, and you need a coach to develop them.
- **Copy editor:** I don't care if you're the best writer in the world, you need a copy editor. Copy editors look for inconsistencies in your story and fix your work so that it reads properly. They aren't changing the bones of your story like a developmental editor, but they are making it much better by looking out for any narrative inconsistencies that are guaranteed to come up in your story. A good copy editor is the

last line of defense between you and the world reading a book that doesn't make sense. You need one you trust implicitly.

- **Proofreader:** A proofreader is the final person who checks over your work before it goes out the door. They are making sure the spelling and grammar are correct, and there are no errors that astute readers will grill you for once the book releases…and trust me, savvy readers will point them out and take great joy in it.
- **Alpha and Beta readers** are not really editors, but I'm putting them here because they are important. These are usually fans and readers who can tell you where your story is lacking. They probably can't tell you how to fix a problem, but they can turn you on to any problems in your book. In general, I think of **alpha readers** as people who read the book before it goes to editing, while **beta readers** read it right before they release. I've had the same beta reader for all my books, my wife, and if she likes it, then I can confidently release the book. She's the last line of defense before releasing a book.

I absolutely don't want a book to go out the door without it being its very best, so I always have at least two editors and a beta reader. After all, my books will be around for a long time, and I want people to find and love them without finding them wanting. Interestingly, it was my editor who told me to add this section, and she was right. Without it, the book would be incomplete. That is the power of a great editor.

Once I finish editing my drafts, my editor then does two passes at revising the manuscript, and I do a revision to address the editor's notes between each of her drafts. Sometimes, she looks over a couple additional things that are still potential problems after the second revision draft. Usually, though, that's it for my editor. I read it over one more time before it goes to the proofreader.

Once my proofreader is done with the book, I read it through one more time and then lay out the print and e-book editions of the book, before sending it to my wife. When she approves, it goes off to my Advance Reader Copy (ARC) team and gets a publishing date.

I don't know if that's helpful, and it's only one person's process, but I find it helpful to study a proven framework and modify it to suit my needs. I hope you find my framework helpful.

THE ART OF BLURB WRITING

Many authors dread writing blurbs, often spending weeks or months agonizing over them or procrastinating entirely. The key to overcoming this paralysis is understanding what a blurb is - and more importantly, what it isn't. A blurb is not a summary of your story; ***it's an emotional hook designed to make readers desperate to know more.***

Writing an effective blurb can feel overwhelming, but having multiple approaches in your toolkit makes the task more manageable. Let's explore ***three distinct methods*** for crafting blurbs that grab readers' attention and drive sales.

The Story Core Method approach, developed by Libbie Hawker, breaks your story down to its essential elements:

1. Identify your main character
2. Define what they want

3. Establish what prevents them from getting it
4. Show how they struggle against this force
5. Hint at whether they succeed or fail

Using *The Matrix* as an example: "Neo, a computer programmer, wants to understand the truth about reality. The machines controlling humanity prevent him from breaking free. When a mysterious group offers him the chance to see the truth, Neo must risk everything to fight against the system - if he can survive becoming humanity's last hope."

This method works particularly well for character-driven stories where the protagonist's journey is central to the narrative.

The **Three-Hook Structure** approach uses a series of escalating hooks followed by deeper context:

1. Open with three ultra-short descriptions (3-6 words each)
2. Follow with 1-2 paragraphs expanding on the core conflict
3. Include who will love the book
4. End with a call to action

For *The Matrix*: "Reality is a lie. Humanity sleeps in chains. One man can wake us all.

Thomas Anderson has always sensed something was wrong with his world. When he discovers humanity is trapped in a vast computer simulation, he must become more than human to set them free.

If you love reality-bending action, profound philosophical questions, and heroes discovering their true potential, this book is perfect for you.

Get it now."

The *Machine Gun Method* uses a rapid-fire combination of setting, emotion, and character: [Setting] + [Verb/Emotion] + [Character] + [Description] [Second Character] + [Description] + [Stakes] [Three Questions]

For *The Matrix*: "A simulated world. Controlled. A hacker discovering everything he knows is a lie. A mysterious rebellion. Fighting impossible odds. With humanity's freedom hanging in the balance. Can he accept the unbearable truth? Will he become something more than human? Is he truly The One?"

Each method serves different types of stories better:

- The Story Core works best for character-focused narratives
- The Three-Hook Structure excels for high-concept or genre fiction
- The Machine Gun Method shines with action-packed or thriller-style stories

Consider writing your blurb using all three methods and seeing which resonates most strongly with your story. ***Sometimes, you might even combine elements from different approaches.*** For instance, you might use the Machine Gun Method's setting introduction, followed by the Story Core's character focus, and end with the Three-Hook Structure's target audience statement.

Remember the core principles that apply *regardless* of method:

- Keep it between 100-250 words
- Focus on emotional connection over plot summary
- Leave questions unanswered to create intrigue

- Speak directly to your target audience

The best way to master blurb writing is to practice all three methods. Try rewriting your favorite books' blurbs using each approach. This exercise helps you understand how different structures can highlight different aspects of the same story.

GETTING A GREAT COVER

One of the most crucial decisions you make in publishing your book is the cover. While it might be tempting to view cover design as simply an artistic choice or to cut corners to save money, **your cover serves as much more than mere decoration**. It's a vital communication tool that helps your book find its intended audience.

Think about the last time you browsed books online or in a bookstore. Before reading a single word of the story, you have likely made split-second decisions about which books might interest you based solely on their covers. **Your potential readers are doing exactly the same thing.** In the few seconds someone spends scanning search results or browsing shelves, your cover needs to instantly communicate not just genre and tone, but the entire reading experience they can expect.

When readers see a cover that doesn't align with genre expectations or appears unprofessional, they assume the writing inside will reflect the same lack of understanding or polish.

This isn't about judging a book by its cover. It's about readers using covers as a reliable shorthand for finding the kinds of stories they enjoy. A romance reader knows what signals to look for in a romance cover, just as a thriller reader can spot a compelling thriller cover from across the room. Really great covers find ways to integrate the colors, items, and themes of the story into their cover, where appropriate.

This is why studying your genre's current visual language is so crucial. **Look at the top 100 books in your category on Amazon.** Note the patterns: How do they use color? What kinds of images do they feature? How is text positioned and styled? These aren't arbitrary choices - they've evolved because they effectively signal to readers "this is the kind of story you're looking for."

A well-chosen pre-made cover that perfectly matches your genre's conventions will serve your book far better than an expensive custom cover that sends the wrong signals.

The real question isn't, "How much should I spend on a cover?" but rather, "How can I ensure my book reaches the readers who will love it?" A cover that clearly signals your genre and attracts your target audience might cost $50 or $500. What matters is its effectiveness as a communication tool. Your goal isn't to have the most beautiful or artistic cover, but to have one that helps the right readers find your book.

Remember that your cover works in tandem with your blurb and sample pages. Together, they create a promise to the reader about the experience they'll have with your book. Breaking that promise is the quickest way to disappoint readers and harm your career as an author.

So when considering your cover options, ask yourself, "Will this help my ideal readers recognize this book as something they want to read?" If you're writing a cozy mystery but your cover screams thriller, you're not just risking lost sales, you're setting yourself up for disappointed readers who wanted something different from what you're offering. The most "beautiful" cover in the world isn't doing its job if it's attracting the wrong readers or failing to attract the right ones.

FINDING THE RIGHT COVER DESIGNER

Think of finding a cover designer like hiring an architect. You need someone who not only has technical skill but also deeply understands the kind of structure you're trying to build. Just as you wouldn't hire a specialist in industrial buildings to design your cozy cottage, you shouldn't hire a romance cover designer for your military science fiction novel.

Start by creating a collection of covers you admire in your genre. **When you find covers that particularly speak to you, look up the designer.** Many authors credit their cover designers in their books' copyright pages or on their websites. This research serves two purposes: it helps you identify designers who excel in your genre, and it gives you concrete examples to share when communicating your vision.

Three main paths exist for finding designers:

- **Pre-made cover designers:** Usually, I don't hire a designer to start from scratch. Instead, I find a pre-made cover that a designer has already made and pay them to customize it for me. This allows me to see the end product and how it will feel to find it for readers. These designers understand genre conventions and often create covers in sets, perfect for series planning. The key is regularly checking their sites as new designs appear, since good covers sell quickly.

- **Mid-range custom designers:** These professionals typically charge $300-800 per cover and often have portfolios specializing in specific genres. They're found through author recommendations, writing forums, and professional marketplaces like Reedsy. Look for designers who showcase multiple covers in your specific genre - not just general book cover work.

- **High-end custom designers:** Starting at $1000+, these designers often work with both traditional publishers and independent authors. They're typically found through industry connections or their own established websites. While expensive, they offer the highest level of customization and often have deep genre expertise.

Cover designers aren't hard to find. They are **literally** announcing themselves on the cover of the book. A good designer isn't just a service provider. They're a partner in your book's success. They should be able to explain their design choices in terms of market expectations and reader psychology. If a designer can't articulate why they make specific choices for your genre, they might not have the expertise you need.

Consider your cover design budget as a marketing investment rather than a production cost. A professionally designed cover that perfectly targets your audience can pay for itself many times over through:

- Higher conversion rates from browsers to buyers
- Better targeted advertising results
- Increased reader trust in your professionalism
- Series recognition leading to stronger follow-on sales

Throughout this book, we've explored how to transform your initial spark of inspiration into a fully realized book that connects with readers. From nurturing and selecting the right ideas, to building compelling characters and worlds, to crafting effective structures for your story, each element plays a crucial role in creating a satisfying reading experience.

But having a great story isn't enough. You need to ensure it reaches the readers who will love it. ***This is where the packaging of your book becomes crucial.*** Your blurb serves as an emotional bridge between your story and your potential readers, creating an irresistible promise about the experience that awaits them. Your cover acts as a visual shorthand, instantly communicating genre and tone to help the right readers recognize your book as something they want to read. And professional formatting ensures that nothing stands between your words and your reader's immersion in the story.

Remember that every decision you make in this process should serve *two* masters: your creative vision and your readers' expectations.

The most beautiful prose won't find its audience without effective packaging, just as the most attractive cover won't satisfy readers if the story inside doesn't deliver on its promises. Success comes from understanding how all these elements work together to create a complete package that attracts and satisfies your target audience.

Most importantly, don't let perfectionism paralyze you. ***Your first book won't be perfect, and that's okay.*** What matters is that you're learning and improving with each story you tell. Start with strong ideas that excite you, develop them with careful attention to craft, and present them professionally to the world. Build your skills one book at a time, always keeping your focus on creating the best possible experience for your readers.

The journey from idea to published book may seem daunting, but broken down into these manageable steps, it becomes an achievable goal. Whether you're crafting your first novel or your fiftieth, these principles remain the same. Keep learning, keep writing, and keep striving to connect with readers who will love your stories.

HOW TO BANK 1,000 PRE-ORDERS FOR YOUR BOOK

I'll be honest, getting 1,000 pre-orders for a book is one of those goals that sounds impressive but can feel downright ridiculous, especially when you're just starting out. I've only hit 1,000 pre-orders once, and frankly, I think it's a bad idea to make that your target early in your career. But people keep asking me how to do it, so I'm finally going to break it down.

In fact, in 2024 we spent $50,000 on audience growth and the #1 best performing ads used some combination of, "Get 1,000 pre-orders."

So, here we go.

This isn't going to be easy, and it probably won't happen the first time you try, but if you're determined to go for it, there are strategies that can help you get there.

Let's get one thing straight off the top.

Pre-orders are **harder** to get than regular sales. Readers don't get instant gratification, so you're asking for more than just their money. You're asking for their patience and trust. Meanwhile, they have access to every book that's ever been released at their fingerprints.

Then, when you add in that if you're reading this you've probably not released many books yet, and now you're asking people to trust an unproven commodity. Even once you release a book it's difficult to get somebody to give you a chance. It's dang near impossible to do so before a book is even released.

If you're starting with a small email list or limited social media reach, the math can feel brutal. On average:

- **Email lists:** Only about 1-2% of subscribers might pre-order your book, even with strong engagement. Honestly, if you had this kind of conversion rate on a fully released book it would be pretty good. So, you'll likely get even lower than this on pre-orders.
- **Social media:** Only about 1-3% of your followers will even see your promotion on social media, and only 1-3% of those will take action.
- **Touchpoints:** Readers typically need 7-12 interactions before they'll take action. That means your message needs to land over and over again.

That's a lot of math that has to math in order for the math to math in your favor. ***This isn't meant to discourage you.*** It's meant to prepare you. If you're a new author, hitting 1,000 pre-orders isn't just about the end goal. It's about using the process to learn, grow your audience, and lay the foundation for future success.

The only reason I think this exercise has any merit is because with every push, you are building your audience, and in order to get 1,000 pre-orders, you're going to have to make a sustained marketing push that will force you to get comfortable with a lot of things that authors tend to shy away from for years.

The best time to market your books is leading up to a launch, so you'll likely grow your audience a lot trying for this big goal.

Pre-orders require **relentless repetition.** People don't make decisions the first time they hear about something. They don't even make decisions the seventh time. The average reader needs 7-12 interactions with your book before they even consider clicking "Buy." That's not because they don't like you or your book. It's because they're busy, distracted, and inundated with options. Your job is to make sure they can't forget about you.

This is the paradox of promotion. *What feels like shouting into the void to you is often the faintest whisper to your readers.* There's a saying in marketing. When you feel like you've said enough, you're only about **5%** of the way there. That means you still have **95%** of your work ahead of you. It's not because you're failing. It's because your audience needs more time, more touchpoints, and more reminders to take action.

I promote my books hard, and I have never had a launch end without somebody commenting that they didn't even know I was launching something. By the end I'm exhausted and sick of talking about my book while my audience has barely tuned in to hear about it.

That means showing up consistently. It means crafting emails that intrigue them, writing posts that make them stop scrolling, and offering them reasons to care. You're not just selling a book. You're selling a connection, an experience, and sometimes, a piece of yourself.

And here's where it gets tricky. The more ambitious your pre-order goal, the more touch points you'll need, and the more platforms you'll have to leverage. If you're aiming for 1,000 pre-orders, you can't just rely on one channel. Your email list, social media, ads, partnerships all have to work together to create the kind of buzz that makes people pay attention.

The mental toll wears on you over the course of a pre-order campaign, but it's nothing compared to **the emotional toll. Pre-order**s require patience. A lot of it. You'll send emails that no one opens. Post on social media and watch the algorithm bury your hard work. Spend hours perfecting an ad only to see it barely convert. It's frustrating, and honestly, it can make you feel like you're shouting into the void.

And to some extent that's exactly what you are doing, except sometimes the void screams back, and that's what we're all hoping will happen *a lot* when we launch something.

FINDING YOUR STRATEGY

Whether you're traditionally published or indie, if your book comes in a specific format like a graphic novel or audiobook, your path to success depends on adapting your strategy to your unique situation.

If you're a traditional author, you'll likely have some support from your publisher, but it's often not enough on its own. Yes, you can use their network to secure retailer placement and influencer support, but it doesn't stop there. You'll have to supplement their efforts by engaging with your personal audience, whether that's through your email list, social media, or local events. Your publisher might not have the bandwidth to give your book the spotlight it deserves, so it's up to you to make it stand out.

You do have a support network when you are traditionally published though, and you should use it. Make your own list of marketing actions and ask for their help. Publishers love when you schedule a book tour or go to conventions after a book releases. They'll often even send books with you at their cost if you go to a conference so your name gets out there. Before a launch, your editor and publicist can work with you to make the most of your network and amplify it with theirs, so make sure to stay in conversation with them.

Most authors sit passively by and wait for the publisher to do things, but if you take your fate into your own hands, your publisher will often match your effort.

For indie authors, you're in full control of your campaign, which is both a challenge and an opportunity. You'll need to take ownership of every aspect, from audience building to outreach. The good news is that you're free to experiment. Try a mix of direct sales, email campaigns, and grassroots efforts to see what works best for your audience.

Your book's format also plays a role in how you approach pre-orders. If you're writing a children's book, your audience isn't the kids. It's their parents, teachers, and librarians. Focus on connecting with these gatekeepers through school outreach, local bookstores, and child-friendly events. If your book is a graphic novel or comic, lean into visual-heavy platforms like Instagram or TikTok, where eye-catching art can grab attention. For audiobooks, podcast appearances and collaborations with popular narrators can make all the difference.

The key is to meet your readers where they are, with strategies that make sense for your specific publishing path and format. The more aligned your campaign is with your book's unique needs, the more effective it will be.

Frankly, if you get 100 pre-orders you should do a happy dance. Getting to 1,000 is mental. So, why do it? Why put yourself through this?

Because every time you send an email or post about your book, you're not just marketing for *this* launch. You're planting seeds for the next one. You're building an audience that will remember you, even if they don't buy this time. You're creating a foundation that will make your future launches easier, faster, and more successful.

And here's the best part: *you don't have to be perfect.* You just have to be persistent. Pre-orders aren't about doing everything flawlessly. They're about showing up again and again, until people can't help but notice.

The truth is, pre-orders require more than most people think they can give. But they also give you something in return: experience, growth, and the beginnings of a loyal readership. And that? That's worth every ounce of effort.

WHY PRE-ORDERS ARE HARD

Pre-orders are a different beast from regular sales, which are hard enough as it is to get right. When you're asking someone to pre-order, you're not just selling a book.

You're selling the promise of a book. Readers don't get instant gratification, and for many, that's a hurdle. They might think, *Why not just wait until it's available?* or *What if I don't like it?* These challenges are amplified if you're a newer author or working with a small audience. Convincing readers to trust you and your story before they've even read a page is no small task.

But pre-orders aren't just about getting sales early. They're about building momentum, creating excitement, and showing your audience why your book is worth their attention. If you can overcome the natural hesitation that comes with pre-orders, you can turn a skeptical reader into a lifelong fan.

Readers hesitate to pre-order for a few reasons, and it's not because they don't like you or your book. It's because pre-ordering is inherently a leap of faith. They're giving you their money now and waiting weeks, or even months, for something in return. They're busy, distracted, and often unfamiliar with how pre-orders work or why they matter. Many readers simply don't understand their pre-order could be the thing that helps a book they love find a bigger audience.

And that's where you come in. It's your job to bridge the gap, to show them why pre-ordering your book isn't just a good idea, it's an exciting opportunity to be part of something special.

When you approach pre-orders, think of it as an opportunity to start a conversation with your readers. Instead of focusing on the transaction, focus on what the pre-order represents. Pre-orders are about trust, exclusivity, and being part of the story before anyone else. They're not just buying a book. They're joining your journey.

Talk to your readers about why pre-orders matter. Let them know how pre-orders influence bookstore orders, retailer visibility, and even how algorithms decide which books to recommend. Let them know that every pre-order is a vote of confidence that helps your book reach more readers. Be transparent, honest, and authentic. When your audience understands the stakes, they'll be more inclined to take that leap.

The waiting period is the main thing that makes pre-orders harder than regular sales, but it's also what makes them special. When readers pre-order, they're choosing to believe in your book before it's even in their hands. Reward that trust by giving them something that makes the wait exciting.

Maybe you share a sneak peek at the first chapter or send exclusive updates about your writing process. Perhaps you offer pre-order bonuses like digital wallpapers, short stories, or behind-the-scenes videos. These extras aren't just perks. They're ways to keep readers engaged and excited while they wait.

For example, imagine telling your audience: *"When you pre-order, you'll get a free bonus scene that takes place after the story ends. It's my thank-you for believing in this book before anyone else."* Suddenly, pre-ordering isn't just about getting a book. It's about being part of something unique.

This is part of the secret sauce to how Kickstarter works to sell books. It's not just about getting the book. It's about getting it early, in a special way, with unique bonuses only available during the campaign. There's no reason you can't bring some of that to your pre-order campaign, even if you choose not to run a crowdfunding campaign.

The most powerful tool you have for overcoming hesitation is your own enthusiasm. If you're excited about your book, that energy will come through in your messaging. Talk about why this story matters to you, what inspired it, and what makes it special. When readers see your passion, they'll want to share it.

It's also important to address the wait directly. Acknowledge that pre-orders require patience but frame it as part of the fun. *"Pre-ordering isn't just about buying a book. It's about being part of the journey. By pre-ordering, you're supporting this story and helping it reach readers around the world."* Give them a reason to feel good about their choice.

BUILD THE CASE FOR YOUR BOOK

A pre-order campaign isn't about shouting, "Buy my book." It's about having a conversation with your readers to show them why your book is worth their attention. Everything you share is another chance to explain what makes your story special. Every day of your campaign is another opportunity to highlight something new and meaningful about your book, gradually building a case that resonates with your audience.

When you first announce your pre-order, the case is simple: *The book is live, and you can be one of the first to get it.* That's your starting point. But as the days go on, you have to keep building on that message. It's exhausting, but it's also supposed to be fun. If it's not fun *for you*, then it won't be fun *for them.*

One day you might talk about what inspired the story. Another, you could share an early review or a behind-the-scenes look at the writing process. Maybe you dive into a character's backstory or offer a sneak peek of the first chapter. Each piece adds depth, helping readers connect with your book in a new way.

The middle of a pre-order campaign is often where things slow down, and that's where your creativity matters most. **Think about what excites you about the book and share that with your readers.** If you're writing a series, remind them why they love this world and what makes this installment special. If it's a standalone, lean into the unique themes or emotional core of the story.

Over time, you build a language with your readers by giving them reasons to love your book. No single interaction will likely push them over the edge, but creating a campaign allows you to find the story that will connect with them.

Your readers aren't all the same. Some will pre-order the moment you announce, while others will need a little more time and nudging. Maybe they're on the fence and need to see a glowing review. Maybe they just need to be reminded a few times because life is busy, and your book hasn't made it to the top of their to-do list. That's why variety matters. Each day of your campaign gives you a chance to catch someone's attention in a new way.

Pre-orders are about more than just selling a book. They're about sharing your enthusiasm, creating anticipation, and showing readers why this story matters, not just to you, but to them. When you approach each day with a fresh perspective and a new piece of your book's heart, you're not just building a case. You're creating an experience that readers will remember.

As a newer author, it's easy to feel like you'll never get anywhere and that you'll always be overshadowed by superstar authors with massive followings, endless resources, and access to the biggest promotional platforms, but ***you have something they don't.*** You can show up for your readers in a way they can't. Your presence is your superpower.

When a superstar author releases a book, their reach might be enormous, but their connection with individual readers is often diluted. They can't respond to every comment, answer every email, or personally thank every reader who supports them.

But you can. Your ability to connect directly with your fans, to make each one feel seen and valued, is a secret weapon that superstar authors can't replicate.

This doesn't just make a difference in your pre-order campaign. It builds a foundation for lasting loyalty. Readers don't just want to buy books. They want to feel connected to the authors who create them. By showing up authentically and consistently, you create relationships that turn casual readers into passionate advocates.

Here's how to use your presence to its fullest potential:

- Respond to comments and emails with genuine enthusiasm. A quick thank-you or thoughtful reply can make a reader's day.

- Engage directly with your audience through live streams, Q&A sessions, or private community spaces. Let them see the person behind the book.
- Share personal insights, behind-the-scenes moments, or even the struggles of the creative process. These glimpses of authenticity resonate deeply with readers.

Your availability and willingness to connect are what make you stand out. Readers might admire superstar authors, but they'll champion *you* because they feel like they know you. Lean into that, and you'll create a reader base that grows not just in numbers but in loyalty and passion.

BUILD A FOUNDATION THAT WORKS FOR YOU

Your path to 1,000 pre-orders has to align with your strengths, your audience, and your book. This is where many authors go wrong. They think they have to do all the things, but that's a ***surefire*** way to burn out. Instead, focus on building a foundation that fits you and your book.

Start by asking yourself where your audience is most likely to be. If you're writing a children's book, you might find your readers through parent groups, teachers, or librarians. If you're writing a comic, your audience is probably hanging out in visual-heavy spaces like Instagram, TikTok, or even niche communities on Discord or Reddit. The key is meeting your readers where they already are, instead of shouting into the void and hoping they find you.

It's not just about being in the right place. It's about creating a consistent message. **Readers need to understand**

why your book matters to them. This is where a lot of authors falter. They think, *I'll just tell people I wrote a book and they'll buy it.* But readers don't care that you wrote a book. They care about what your book will do for them. Will it make them laugh? Teach them something? Transport them to a world they've never seen before? Your job is to answer those questions before they even ask.

Even the most personal books don't succeed because of what the author went through. They succeed because of how the reader is able to use the book as a conduit to process their own transformation. It's not really about you at all.

You also need to think about the tools and tactics that work best for you. Maybe you love email and feel confident crafting newsletters that people actually want to open. Or maybe you're better at connecting through video and can build an audience by posting short, engaging clips on TikTok. Lean into your strengths. There's no one-size-fits-all approach, so don't force yourself into a strategy that doesn't feel natural.

The hardest part is staying consistent. **Building a foundation takes time.** It might mean spending weeks building a blog in the same vein as your book to attract the right audience. Or it might mean slowly growing your email list by offering free resources that connect with your book's theme. Whatever it is, it won't happen overnight. But the work you put in now will pay off when it's time to launch.

This is what separates authors who succeed from those who give up. It'**s not about having the biggest budget or the fanciest tools.** It's about showing up every day and doing the work. Not because you'll see results right away, but because you know the results are coming.

Building a foundation that works for you isn't about doing it all. It's about doing what works, consistently, with patience and persistence. Because when you find the right combination of strategies, your audience will notice. And when they do, they'll start to trust you. That's when the pre-orders start rolling in.

FIND THE RIGHT READERS BY LISTENING AND TESTING

The hardest part of any pre-order campaign isn't about finding readers. Readers are everywhere. There are literally billions of them around the world.

The trick lies in finding the right readers. The ones who will not only pre-order your book but connect with it so deeply that they tell their friends about it, leave reviews, and come back for your next launch. So, how do you figure out who those readers are and what they want? It starts with listening and testing.

If you've launched a book before, even if it was a small launch, you already have some data to work with to give you insights. Who bought it? Who shared it? What did they say in reviews or comments? If you don't have a previous book, think about other ways readers have interacted with you. What content gets the most engagement on your social media? Which email newsletters do people reply to? ***This isn't just feedback. It's a map to understanding your audience.***

If you don't even have this level of data, then it's time to start testing. You don't need a massive audience to start learning what resonates. If you're active on social media, post about different aspects of your book, like an intriguing character, a unique world, or a compelling theme. See what gets the most attention. If you send emails, try including a question or sharing a snippet from your book. Watch for replies, clicks, and engagement. These small experiments will help you refine your messaging and understand what your readers care about most.

If you don't have much of an audience yet, look at similar authors in your genre. What are their readers excited about? Read their reviews, check their social media, and pay attention to the conversations happening in their spaces. You're not copying them; you're learning what resonates with the people you're trying to reach.

Your readers are out there, talking about books like yours. The trick is finding where those conversations are happening. If you're writing a cozy mystery, check out book clubs and Facebook groups where mystery lovers gather. Writing fantasy? Dive into Reddit threads, Discord servers, or TikTok hashtags where readers share their favorite tropes and authors. ***Don't just observe, join the conversations, not as a salesperson, but as someone who genuinely loves what they love.***

This will teach you the language of your reader that you can deploy when you're ready to launch your own book. Not only will you know the stakeholders, but you'll be able to speak with them in a language they understand.

Readers want stories that make them feel something, solve a problem, or fill a gap in their lives. Your job is to find the overlap between what they're looking for and what your book offers. Maybe your fantasy novel gives them the immersive escape they crave after a stressful day. Maybe your nonfiction book solves a problem they've been struggling with. It's not about selling them a book. It's about connecting your story to their lives.

One of the most direct ways to find out what your readers want is to ask them. If you already have an audience, send out a short survey or ask questions in your newsletter or on social media. What are they looking for in a book? What frustrates them about the genre? What themes, characters, or settings make them pick up a story? If you're just starting out, these questions can still be valuable in genre-specific groups or forums. The key is not to pitch, but to listen.

One of my favorite strategies is to reach out personally to my best readers and ask to meet with them for 30 minutes. **Surveys are fine, but interviewing ten of your best readers will tell you more than getting 1,000 surveys ever could.**

Finding the right readers and understanding what they want isn't a one-time task. It's an ongoing process of listening, testing, and refining. The more you pay attention to your audience, the better you'll get at recognizing what works, and the closer you'll get to building a loyal readership that keeps coming back.

The best time to start this work is way before you need it. So, even if you're years away from launching a book, this kind of work can help you build the resources to use when you do need them.

CRAFT MESSAGING THAT CONNECTS

Talking about your book isn't just about telling people what it's about. It's about showing them why it matters to them. **Readers don't buy books because they exist.** They buy books because they see something in the story that resonates with their lives, their emotions, or their imaginations. Crafting messaging that connects is about building that bridge between your story and their world.

The first step is speaking their language. E*very audience has a way of thinking and talking about the books they love.* If your readers rave about "emotional roller coasters" or "unforgettable heroes" in their favorite stories, use those words when you describe your book. If they love specific tropes like "grumpy/sunshine romance" or "chosen one adventures," lean into those familiar hooks.

It's not about mimicking what's trendy. It's about showing readers that your book fits into the kinds of stories they already love while offering something uniquely yours.

Readers also want to know what's in it for them. They don't just want to hear about a magical quest or a strong female lead. They want to know how your book will make them feel. Will it leave them breathless with suspense? Will it inspire them to believe in their strengths? Will it make them laugh when they need it most? Your messaging needs to focus on the experience your book delivers, not just its features.

For example, instead of saying, *This book has a strong female lead,* you might say, *Meet a heroine who overcomes impossible odds and inspires you to do the same.* Or, instead of saying, *This guide is packed with tips for entrepreneurs,* try, *Discover strategies to grow your business without burning out.* The shift is subtle but powerful—it's about centering the reader and their journey.

Connection also happens through authenticity. Readers don't just want to know about your book. They want to know about you. What inspired you to write this story? What personal experiences shaped its characters or themes? These little glimpses into your journey create trust and make your campaign feel real. **It's not just another book to them. It's your book.**

At the same time, your messaging should spark curiosity. Don't give everything away in one breath. Share an intriguing quote, pose a question the book answers, or tease a moment of high tension. Let readers wonder about the world you've created, the mysteries within, or the characters they'll meet. Curiosity keeps them engaged and draws them closer to clicking that pre-order button.

One of the hardest parts of crafting messaging is keeping it fresh throughout a campaign. You'll need to repeat the core message but find new ways to say it. One day you might focus on the emotional heart of the story, another day on an enthusiastic early review, and the next on a fun pre-order perk. The trick is to keep the energy alive while always driving home why this book deserves their attention.

No matter how creative your messaging gets, it should always end with a clear call to action: pre-order now. Readers need simple, direct instructions on what to do next. Include a link, make the ask clear, and give them a reason to act today instead of waiting until later.

Crafting messaging that connects takes effort, but it's what transforms a potential reader into a pre-order. ***It's not just about selling a book. It's about creating a connection.***

When your words reflect their hopes, dreams, or desires, readers will feel seen. And when they feel seen, they're far more likely to pre-order your story and make it part of their world. Moreso, it's about becoming an avatar for your reader's transformation, even if you're writing fiction, and then proving that your book will help them achieve that transformation, even if that's just to live in another world for a while and forget their problems.

MAKE EVERY INTERACTION COUNT

A pre-order campaign isn't just about big moments like launch day or final reminders. It's about the smaller interactions in between that add up over time. Every email you send, every social post you share, and every conversation you have is an opportunity to build excitement for your book. The key is making each one meaningful.

Think about how often you see ads or promotions and scroll past without a second thought. Your readers are no different. They're busy, distracted, and bombarded with noise. That's why you can't just announce your book and expect people to rush to pre-order. Instead, you need to create moments that stop them in their tracks and make them think, *This is something I don't want to miss.*

One way to make interactions count is by showing readers something they didn't know they needed. Maybe it's a sneak peek at a compelling scene or a glimpse into your creative process. Maybe it's a behind-the-scenes photo of your workspace or a heartfelt post about why this story means so much to you. *When you invite readers into your world, you're not just asking them to pre-order a book. You're asking them to join the journey.*

Another way to stand out is by keeping things personal. A generic, one-size-fits-all message won't cut it. Your readers want to feel like you're talking directly to them. If you're emailing your list, start with a personal anecdote or a note of gratitude for their support. On social media, engage in the comments or respond to DMs. These small gestures make people feel seen, and when people feel seen, they're more likely to invest in your book.

But let's be real, keeping up with every platform, email, and interaction can be exhausting. *That's why it's important to work smarter, not harder.* Focus on the channels where your audience is most active and double down on what's working. If you're getting great engagement on Instagram, lean into that. If your email click rates are climbing, test different formats to see what resonates most. You don't have to do everything. You just have to do the right things well.

Ideally, if it's going well, you can hire people to fill in the gaps where you aren't strong, like a virtual assistant, PR person, or even an ads expert. The right team can amplify your exposure while reducing your anxiety.

It's also worth remembering that not every interaction will result in an immediate pre-order, and that's okay. *Marketing is a cumulative effort.* One post might plant a seed, another might nurture curiosity, and yet another might finally push someone to click "pre-order." Together, these moments build the momentum that makes your campaign successful.

Finally, don't forget to have fun with it. *If you're excited about sharing your book, that energy will come through in every interaction.* Readers want to feel your enthusiasm. They want to believe in the story you're telling, Not just in the book, either, but in your campaign as a whole. So, let them see your passion. Let them feel why this matters.

Every interaction you have is a chance to connect, to share, and to invite readers into the world of your book. Make those moments count, and over time, you'll see the results add up.

TURN CURIOSITY INTO COMMITMENT

Curiosity gets readers interested, but commitment gets them to pre-order. The gap between *Oh, that looks interesting* and *I need to have this book right now* is where many campaigns falter. Turning curiosity into commitment means giving readers the final push they need to click "pre-order."

The first step is understanding that curiosity is just the beginning. *When a reader stumbles across your book for the first time, they might be intrigued by the cover or a brief description. But curiosity fades quickly if you don't follow up with something more substantial.* That's where your messaging comes in. You need to build on their initial interest by showing them why your book isn't just intriguing. It's unmissable.

One of the most effective ways to deepen curiosity is to give readers a taste of what's inside. Share the opening chapter, a character profile, or a key scene. If your book is nonfiction, offer a small excerpt that solves a specific problem or shares a powerful insight. Think of this as a "try before you buy" moment. It's your chance to prove that the story or content lives up to their expectations.

Another strategy is to use social proof. Readers are more likely to commit when they see that other people are already excited about your book. Share early reviews, testimonials, or even comments from readers who've pre-ordered. If you're engaging with your audience on social media, highlight their enthusiasm. *"I just pre-ordered and can't wait to read!"* is the kind of validation that can tip a hesitant reader into action.

Scarcity and urgency are also powerful motivators. Give readers a reason to act now rather than later. Maybe it's a limited-time bonus, like a free short story or a behind-the-scenes video for early pre-orders. Maybe it's a countdown to the end of a special deal or perk. Urgency creates focus, and focus drives decisions.

The most important factor in turning curiosity into commitment is clarity. Readers need to know exactly what they're getting and how to get it. Make your call to action clear and easy to follow. Use direct language like, Pre-order *now and get instant access to [specific bonus]*. Include a direct link to the pre-order page, and make sure your messaging is consistent across every platform.

Curiosity opens the door, but commitment is what gets readers through it. By combining intrigue, social proof, urgency, and clarity, you can turn casual interest into excitement, and excitement into action.

BUILD COMPLEMENTARY CONTENT AND COMMUNITY THROUGH COLLABORATIONS

When you're launching a pre-order campaign, you can't do it alone. Collaborations are one of the most effective ways to expand your reach, tap into new audiences, and create excitement around your book. But it's not just about teaming up with anyone. The best collaborations feel authentic, serve both parties, and provide something valuable for readers.

So how do you find the right opportunities, and what steps can you take to make these partnerships successful?

Collaborations don't have to begin with strangers. **Start with the people you already know, like fellow authors, bloggers, podcasters, or creators in your genre.** If you've been part of an author group, attended events, or even had casual interactions on social media, reach out and start a conversation. The key is to ask yourself, *What value can we create together?*

For example:

- If you're writing nonfiction, partner with another expert in your field for a co-hosted webinar.
- A romance author could team up with another writer to create a "sneak peek" bundle featuring the first chapters of both books.
- For comics or graphic novels, connect with an artist for an exclusive piece of artwork to share with both of your audiences.

Your pitch doesn't need to be complicated. Something as simple as, *"I love your work, and I think we share a similar audience. Would you be interested in collaborating to help promote our books?"* can open the door to possibilities.

If your current network feels limited, it's time to branch out. Start by asking, *Where do my ideal readers spend their time online?* and look for creators who are already engaging with those audiences. This might include:

- **Authors in your genre:** Check Amazon bestsellers, Goodreads lists, or review sites to find authors writing for the same audience.
- **Podcasters and YouTubers:** Search for shows that cater to your book's themes or niche. If you've written a thriller, look for true crime podcasts. If it's a children's book, parenting channels might be a perfect fit.
- **Influencers and bloggers:** Follow hashtags, TikTok trends, or genre-specific blogs to find creators who are actively engaging with your readers.

Once you've identified potential collaborators, spend some time engaging with their content. Comment on posts, share their work, or leave a thoughtful review. When you eventually reach out, they'll recognize your name, and you'll already have established a positive connection.

Once you've identified potential collaborators, the next step is reaching out with a clear and compelling pitch. Keep it simple and focus on how the partnership benefits both sides. For example:

- *"I'm launching a fantasy novel, and I'd love to collaborate with you on a joint giveaway. I*

could offer a free copy of my book, and we could cross-promote to our audiences."
- *"I see you run a great podcast about parenting. I'm launching a children's book and would love to come on your show to talk about storytelling for kids."*
- *"I'm putting together a newsletter swap for indie romance authors. Would you be interested in sharing my book in your newsletter? I'd be happy to do the same for yours."*

Be respectful of their time and make it as easy as possible for them to participate. Provide pre-written content, clear instructions, and a timeline to make collaboration effortless.

Honestly, one of the biggest lessons I've learned in finding collaborators is to organize things, instead of just joining them. **People naturally gravitate toward being part of something bigger, but few want to take on the effort of leading.** If you're willing to be the organizer, you'll find others lining up to join you.

Start by thinking about what would excite your ideal readers and collaborators. A multi-author giveaway, a themed blog series, or a shared social media event can bring attention not just to your book but to everyone involved. For example:

- A romance author might organize a Valentine's Day "Books We Love" giveaway with exclusive content from multiple authors.
- A fantasy writer could host a "World-building Week," featuring interviews, live Q&As, or blog posts from other authors in the genre.

- A children's book creator might arrange a "Family Reading Challenge" with printables and activities shared by collaborators.

These events don't have to be complicated. Even a small, well-planned initiative can generate excitement and create buzz. The magic is in bringing people together around a shared theme, idea, or goal.

But how do you find the right people to collaborate with? Start by looking at your existing network. **Fellow authors, bloggers, or illustrators you've worked with before are great places to begin.** If you're unsure, explore spaces where your ideal readers and creators gather. Facebook groups, Reddit threads, and Discord servers tied to your genre or niche are gold mines for discovering potential partners. Engage authentically in these communities, not as someone pushing your book, but as a fellow enthusiast.

When you're ready to reach out, your pitch doesn't have to be perfect. It just needs to focus on what's in it for them. People are busy, and your collaborators will want to know that your idea is worth their time. Say something like:

- *"I'm putting together a joint giveaway for fantasy authors, and I think your book would be a perfect fit. Here's how it would work..."*
- *"I loved your recent blog post on [topic]. I'm organizing a series of guest posts on the theme of resilience in fiction—would you be interested in contributing?"*

Be clear about the value they'll get, whether that's exposure to a new audience, exclusive perks for their readers, or the chance to connect with other creators. Make it easy for them to say yes by providing clear details, pre-written content, or specific timelines.

Organizing something cool doesn't just benefit your collaborators, it also positions you as a leader in your niche. When you're the one creating opportunities, you become someone others want to align with. And even if you're starting small, these partnerships will grow with time.

Collaboration isn't just a nice-to-have. It's a cornerstone of building a successful pre-order campaign. By finding the right partners, creating value together, and engaging authentically, you can turn your book launch into a shared celebration that reaches far beyond your existing audience.

MOBILIZE YOUR AMBASSADORS

The most powerful advocates for your book aren't strangers. They're the readers who already love what you do. We call these superfans your *street team*, and the people on it your **ambassadors**, the people who are excited to spread the word about your book because they genuinely believe in it. When you mobilize them effectively, they can amplify your campaign far beyond what you could do alone.

Your ambassadors are the readers who consistently show up for you. They comment on your posts, reply to your emails, and share your updates with their friends. You don't need a massive following to mobilize ambassadors. A small, engaged group or even 5-10 enthusiastic people can have a huge impact.

Start by reaching out to your existing audience:

- Ask your email list or social media followers if they'd like to join a special pre-order team.
- Look for readers who've left glowing reviews or sent you enthusiastic messages. These are the people who already care about your work and are likely to help.

Keep it personal. A direct message or email saying, *"I'm putting together a small team to help spread the word about my new book. Would you like to be part of it?"* can go a long way.

Once you've recruited your ambassadors, **make it easy for them to promote your book.** Provide pre-written content, eye-catching graphics, and clear instructions for sharing. For example:

- **Social media posts:** Share-ready captions and images they can post on Instagram, Facebook, or Twitter/X.
- **Email templates:** A short, friendly email they can send to friends or book clubs, recommending your book.
- **Exclusive content:** Offer ambassadors sneak peeks, bonus chapters, or behind-the-scenes updates to share with their networks.

The goal is to remove as much friction as possible. If they don't have to create content from scratch, they're more likely to follow through. However, it's also a good idea to encourage your most enthusiastic, savvy fans to remix their own promotional efforts so social media platforms think that there's a bunch of people talking about your book at once and help amplify you.

While many superfans are happy to help for free, ***offering small rewards can boost participation and enthusiasm.*** Think of incentives that align with their interests:

- **Exclusive perks:** Early access to your book, signed copies, or personalized thank-you notes.
- **Recognition:** A shoutout in your book's acknowledgments or a spotlight in your newsletter.
- **Contests:** Offer prizes for ambassadors who refer the most pre-orders or drive the most social media engagement.

The key is to make them feel valued and appreciated. ***When your ambassadors see that their efforts matter, they'll be even more motivated to help.*** Make sure to give regular updates; keep them engaged and excited. Send a weekly email or set up a private group (like a Facebook group or Discord server) where you can share campaign milestones, answer questions, and celebrate wins together.

For example:

- Share progress: *"We're halfway to our pre-order goal—thank you for your amazing support!"*
- Highlight individual contributions: *"Shoutout to Sarah for sharing our book on Instagram and bringing in 10 pre-orders!"*
- Provide ongoing resources: New graphics, updated social media captions, or fresh ideas for promotion.

By keeping your ambassadors in the loop, you'll maintain their momentum throughout the campaign.

Mobilizing ambassadors isn't just about this pre-order campaign. **It's about building a community that will**

support you for years to come. Stay connected with your superfans after the campaign ends. Send them thank-you messages, give them a sneak peek at your next project, or invite them to be part of future launches.

When your ambassadors feel like they're truly part of your journey, they'll continue to advocate for you, helping you grow your audience with every new book.

Mobilizing your ambassadors is one of the most rewarding parts of running a pre-order campaign. *It's not just about selling books.* It's about creating a team of passionate supporters who believe in your work as much as you do. Together, you can turn excitement into action, transforming your book into something readers can't wait to talk about.

LEVERAGE PROMO-STACKING TO DOMINATE ATTENTION

Authors often suffer from a severe lack of funds, especially when it comes to their early launches. Plus, they *hate* doing promotion, even if they simultaneously wrote a book *and* put their name on the cover.

If you really want to be invisible, why is your name on the cover, though? Why is your picture *and* bio inside the book? Why even release a book of your words when you could have left it on your hard drive or deleted it? It's okay to want to be beloved by lots of people, but you have to get over yourself. **Writing a book is an inherently self-aggrandizing, vain act…and that's okay.**

If an author can get over themselves, they will only book a few promos spaced out from each other that end up getting lost in the din of everything else. ***One way to combat that is to focus all your promotion around a short period of time*** and concentrate all your efforts, both organic and paid, around it so that all your promotional efforts amplify each other.

We call this promo stacking, and it's amazing for authors on a budget who want to maximize every dollar.

Promo stacking works because it capitalizes on repetition and is predicated on the premise that if a reader is on one email list, they are probably on several others about the same topic. Since the human brain suffers from recency bias, it's easy to short-circuit it into believing you're a much bigger deal than you are if you can flood the market with your work on a bunch of channels at once. Basically, ***the more closely packed people see your book, the more they will remember it. The more they remember it, the more likely they are to take action and pre-order it.***

The idea is to flood the channels your readers use with your book for a short, intense period. When readers see your campaign across multiple touchpoints, they can't help but notice, trust, and get curious.

Start by centering your promotional efforts around one big event, like a BookBub Featured Deal, and layer additional promotions to amplify its impact. The goal? Create a short-term, high-intensity campaign where your book shows up *everywhere* your target readers look.

Here's how a stacked promo strategy works:

1. **Anchor your campaign with a big event:** Schedule a high-impact promotion, like a BookBub Featured Deal, a Chirp audiobook

promo, or an influencer partnership, as the centerpiece of your campaign. This becomes the focal point that everything else revolves around.
2. **Layer in supporting promotions:** Surround the big event with additional efforts, like newsletter swaps, smaller promo sites like Bargain Booksy or Fussy Librarian, and social media ads. These amplify the visibility created by your anchor event.
3. **Extend the impact:** Use countdowns and follow-ups to maximize the momentum created by your stacked efforts, keeping readers engaged even after the peak.
4. **Coordinate your messaging:** Every piece of your campaign should tie back to the anchor event. Use consistent branding and repeat your core message across all channels.

Promo stacking creates a snowball effect. Smaller promotions prime your audience, the anchor event delivers a massive spike in visibility, and post-event efforts sustain momentum to make it feel like your book is *the* thing everyone's talking about, creating urgency and trust.

This approach works because it respects how people make decisions. *Remember, readers often need 7–12 touchpoints before they buy, and promo stacking ensures those touchpoints happen in quick succession.* By combining strategic timing with focused intensity, you can maximize your pre-order campaign's impact and drive real results.

TRACK YOUR PROGRESS AND REFINE YOUR APPROACH

Running a pre-order campaign is like climbing a mountain. You don't reach the summit in one leap. Instead, you break it into smaller milestones and celebrate each step along the way. ***Every 100 pre-orders is a mini-goal that helps you gauge your progress, refine your strategy, and stay motivated.*** By tracking your campaign in real time and focusing on actionable metrics, you'll not only make the journey less overwhelming but also more effective.

Hitting 1,000 pre-orders might seem daunting, but breaking it into smaller goals makes it manageable. Each milestone represents a chance to test, learn, and optimize your approach. Here's a roadmap:

PRE-ORDERS 1-100: WARM LEADS AND LOW-HANGING FRUIT

- **Focus:** Your inner circle. This includes friends, family, superfans, and your email list. These are the people who already know and love your work.
- **Metrics:** Track email open rates, click-through rates (CTR), and conversions from your direct audience.
- **Strategy:**
    - Send a personal email to your most engaged readers.
    - Offer an exclusive early bird bonus for the first 50-100 pre-orders to create urgency.
    - Use direct outreach like DMs, personal notes, or in-person asks to engage your core supporters.

PRE-ORDERS 101-300: EXPANDING REACH

- **Focus:** Engaging your social media followers and reaching casual fans.
- **Metrics:** Look at engagement rates on social media posts (likes, shares, comments) and ad click-thru rates.
- **Strategy:**
    - Use teaser content like sneak peeks, behind-the-scenes videos, or excerpts to build excitement.
    - Start layering in paid ads with low budgets to test messaging and audiences.
    - Begin newsletter swaps with authors who write for a similar audience.

PRE-ORDERS 301-600: BUILDING MOMENTUM

- **Focus:** Expanding into new audiences and leveraging partnerships.
- **Metrics:** Measure referral traffic from newsletter swaps, social shares, and collaborations.
- **Strategy:**
    - Partner with other authors for joint promotions, like group giveaways or bundles.
    - Ramp up your ad spend with refined targeting based on earlier results.
    - Pitch guest blog posts or podcast appearances to reach readers outside your immediate audience.

PRE-ORDERS 601-900: ATTENTION DOMINATION

- **Focus:** Making your campaign inescapable.

- **Metrics:** Track impressions, ad frequency, and total traffic to your pre-order page.
- **Strategy:**
    - Execute a promo-stacking strategy by concentrating ads, social posts, and newsletter updates into a single, high-intensity week.
    - Use urgency-driven messaging, such as *"Only 3 days left to claim pre-order bonuses!"*
    - Highlight social proof, share testimonials, reviews, or quotes from early readers.

PRE-ORDERS 901-1,000: THE FINAL PUSH

- **Focus:** Creating urgency and exclusivity.
- **Metrics:** Track daily conversions and bounce rates to identify what's working.
- **Strategy:**
    - Offer a last-minute bonus or limited-time perk for pre-orders in the final stretch.
    - Use countdowns and reminders on all platforms: *"Just 48 hours left to pre-order!"*
    - Engage ambassadors and superfans to amplify your message, asking them to share and promote one last time.

Not all numbers tell the same story. In the middle of a pre-order campaign, it's easy to get lost in surface-level metrics like how many people liked your post or how many followers you gained last week. But those numbers don't necessarily translate to results. What really matters is understanding what drives pre-orders, and focusing on those metrics can make the difference between a successful campaign and one that falls flat.

The first number you should pay attention to is your **conversion rate**. This is the clearest indicator of how effectively your messaging is working. If readers are clicking through your emails, ads, or social media posts but not completing the pre-order, it's a sign something needs to change. Maybe your pre-order page isn't convincing enough, or your call to action isn't clear. On the other hand, a strong conversion rate tells you that your audience is not just interested, they're invested.

Next, look at your **traffic sources**. Where are your pre-orders coming from? Are readers finding you through your email list, social media ads, or collaborations with other authors? Tools like Google Analytics or email tracking can help you pinpoint which channels are driving results. If you notice that one source is outperforming the others, you can double down on what's working and allocate your resources more effectively.

Finally, pay close attention to **engagement**. Are people opening your emails, clicking your links, and interacting with your posts? High engagement is a sign that your messaging is resonating, even if it hasn't yet translated into pre-orders. On the flip side, low engagement might mean it's time to rethink your approach. Are your subject lines intriguing enough? Are your social media posts grabbing attention within the first few seconds? Engagement is the bridge between awareness and action, and it's a metric you can't afford to ignore.

Tracking these numbers isn't just about gathering data. It's about making informed decisions. When you know what's working and what isn't, you can pivot in real time, refining your strategy to maximize impact. Every click, pre-order, and interaction tells a story. Your job is to listen to what those numbers are saying and use them to create a campaign that resonates with your audience and drives results.

KEEP THE MOMENTUM ALIVE AFTER YOUR LAUNCH

A successful pre-order campaign doesn't end when your book is released. The work you've put into generating excitement, building relationships, and engaging your audience can carry over into the next phase of your book's life. Post-launch momentum is about turning the energy of your pre-order campaign into long-term connections, ongoing sales, and a foundation for your future projects.

When your campaign ends, don't quietly move on, celebrate! Whether you hit your goal or came close, take a moment to recognize the achievement and share it with your audience. A public thank-you not only shows gratitude but also reinforces the community you've built. Share your results in an email or social media post:

- *"Thank you to everyone who pre-ordered! We hit [goal], and I couldn't have done it without you."*
- Include a behind-the-scenes look at what the pre-order campaign meant to you or share stories about how readers' support made a difference.

This isn't just about closure. It's about showing readers that their involvement mattered, building goodwill for future campaigns.

Your pre-order buyers are more than just early supporters. They're your most engaged readers and the foundation of your future success. These are the people who believed in your book before they could even hold it in their hands. Now that it's out in the world, this is your chance to deepen that connection and turn casual fans into lifelong advocates.

Start by reaching out personally, if you can. A simple thank-you email or message can go a long way. Let them know how much their support meant to you and make it clear that they're part of something special. Whether it's a heartfelt note or a short video, that personal touch makes readers feel valued and appreciated.

Next, invite them into your world. A private Facebook group, Discord server, or other community space can give your readers a place to connect, not just with you, but with each other. This transforms your audience into a community, a space where they can share their enthusiasm for your work, swap recommendations, and celebrate your book together. ***When readers feel like insiders, they're more likely to stick around for your next project.***

But don't stop there. Give them something extra. Exclusive bonuses, like deleted scenes, additional chapters, or behind-the-scenes content, keep the excitement alive. Maybe you share a map of your fantasy world, a playlist you listened to while writing, or a video tour of your writing space. These extras don't just reward your pre-order buyers. They reinforce their decision to support you and remind them why they were excited in the first place.

Your pre-order campaign isn't just about sales. It's about proving that your book has an audience. Those pre-order numbers are more than a milestone; they're a tool you can use to create new opportunities. Retailers and libraries pay attention to strong pre-order campaigns. Use your stats to pitch better placement or convince a bookstore to stock more copies of your book.

You can also leverage your success to attract influencers, reviewers, or promotional partners. If you can say, *"My book hit 500 pre-orders before launch,"* that's a compelling story that makes others want to be part of your success. **Early reviews from pre-order buyers can also become powerful testimonials**, helping you build credibility as you promote your book to new readers.

Remember that releasing your book is just the beginning. A strong launch is important, but what happens after can make or break its long-term success. Post-launch promotions help you maintain visibility and attract new readers who may have missed your pre-order campaign.

Keep the energy going by scheduling ads or features on platforms like BookBub, Bargain Booksy, or similar promo sites. *These can give your book a second wind and bring in readers who are still discovering it.* Continue engaging with your audience through email and social media. Share reviews, milestones, or personal reflections about what the launch means to you. Show your readers that the story doesn't end with the pre-order. It's still unfolding every day.

Collaborate with other authors in your genre to cross-promote your books. Whether it's a joint giveaway, a shared blog post, or a bundle deal, these partnerships keep your book in front of fresh audiences while building relationships with fellow creators.

The excitement you created during your pre-order campaign doesn't have to fade. When readers see you showing up consistently, sharing your passion, celebrating milestones, and continuing to connect, they'll remember why they pre-ordered in the first place. And when your next book comes out, they'll be ready to join you again.

The goal isn't just to sell one book. It's to build a loyal audience that grows with you. By valuing your readers, leveraging your campaign's success, and keeping the momentum alive, you can turn your pre-order campaign into a launchpad for your career.

After your campaign, take time to reflect. What worked? What didn't? What surprised you? Document your process, including the strategies that delivered the best results and the ones that fell flat. **This isn't just about learning for the future.** It's about giving yourself credit for what you accomplished. Every campaign, successful or not, is a step forward in understanding your audience and growing as an author.

A pre-order campaign is more than a sales strategy. **It's a way to connect with readers, build excitement, and set the stage for your long-term success.** When you keep the momentum alive after launch, you're not just selling a book. You're building a career. And that's a story worth telling again and again.

Write Irresistible Books that Readers Devour

THE STORY BEYOND THE PAGE

By now, you've seen how each part of storytelling, whether it's character, world, theme, pacing, or marketing, can weave into a seamless whole. You've learned to anchor your work in a solid story center, build interwoven elements that reflect or contrast one another, manage your narrative's growth, layer information for maximum effect, and maintain cohesion all the way through to the final page (and beyond).

Yet no matter how finely you tune your outline or how masterfully you juggle character arcs and plot twists, a deeper truth emerges: **your story doesn't live in isolation; it lives in the hearts of your readers.** The journey you set on paper becomes real when it resonates with the very human yearnings that Theodora Taylor calls universal fantasies. And the way you deliver on those yearnings, from the first foreshadowing to the final reveal, determines whether your book is just another piece of entertainment or an experience readers carry with them long after they finish.

In our discussions, we've repeatedly returned to the notion that a story's finale should feel both **surprising and inevitable**. If your ending leaves readers confused or disappointed, you're missing an opportunity to create that satisfying click where every hint and setup suddenly aligns.

This sense of inevitability doesn't mean your plot must be predictable; it means you've laid the groundwork so thoroughly that once the climax arrives, readers see it as the natural conclusion of all that came before.

At the same time, the most powerful endings often contain a final twist of perspective or "turn of the phrase," much like the way Taylor Swift might change a lyric in the third verse to reframe the entire song. When your characters find themselves returning to a place they thought they understood, you're revealing how profoundly the journey has transformed them. Whether that's a literal return to the "ordinary world" or an emotional homecoming to the people and beliefs that matter most, these moments showcase the story's heartbeat: **meaningful change**.

A cohesive narrative doesn't cease to exist the moment readers close the book or hear "The End." Your goal is to create a world and a cast of characters so alive in the reader's imagination that they want to linger there. They might scour your website or newsletter for behind-the-scenes trivia, or chat with other fans in online groups, or flip back to reread favorite passages. In that sense, your novel doesn't simply end; it continues to resonate in the minds of those who connected with it.

This is precisely why **marketing** shouldn't be an afterthought. When you carry the same emotional depth and pacing mastery into your promotional efforts you blur the line between the world on the page and the community around it. Readers respond not just because you "shout" effectively, but because you invite them into a space that feels like a natural extension of the story they love.

THE COHESIVE AUTHOR

Throughout these chapters, we've referenced how film, music, and television approach narrative arcs and emotional payoffs. Whether it's the slow buildup of tension in a streaming series, the carefully plotted set-piece structure of an action blockbuster, or the thematically consistent arc of a concept album, each medium teaches us how modern audiences absorb stories:

1. **Set clear emotional stakes early.** The first scene or "prologue" can act like a microcosm of the entire experience, offering a hint of your style, your world's texture, and your central conflict.
2. **Allow for breathers.** Scenes and sequels, high-action moments and quieter reflections, big set pieces and intimate dialogues—pacing thrives on contrast.
3. **Twist the rules halfway through.** In "Act Two," shift expectations so your protagonist (and readers) realize they're playing a different game than they thought.
4. **Deliver a finale that feels both earned and profound.** Mirror your opening in some way, giving closure or revelation that "echoes" the beginning, but from a place of growth.

When you apply these lessons across your entire creative process—*writing* and *marketing*—you build a career that resonates. Readers pick up one of your stories, follow you to your next release, and gradually understand that whether you're writing a sweeping fantasy epic or a contemporary romance, you never lose sight of what makes storytelling special: the emotional bond forged between you and your audience.

At the end of the day, your books aren't mere commodities; they're artifacts of your deeper obsessions, hopes, and creative instincts.

You weave in universal fantasies, break hearts in Act Two, and orchestrate final triumphs (or tragedies) in Act Three, all because you believe in the power of story to transform a reader's internal landscape. When you share your creative struggles or point out subtle Easter eggs in a newsletter, you do more than sell books, **you invite readers to reflect on their own lives, to find bits of themselves in your characters, to root for hope in dark times.**

That's a privilege and a responsibility. Every new book or marketing message is another chance to speak to your readers' needs, yearnings, and fears. It's also a chance to refine your craft, to keep pushing your own boundaries, and to approach each story with the mindset that it might become somebody's favorite.

Now that you've gathered insights on cohesive storytelling, emotional pacing, archetypal triggers, and authentic marketing, the question is simple: **Where do you go from here?** You can revise your current manuscript through this lens, layering in depth and resonance. Or perhaps you'll plan a fresh story using a more deliberate structure from the start. You might even experiment with how you reveal your plot's inciting incident or how you orchestrate a "dark night of the soul" moment that's not just big and loud but also cuts to the core of your protagonist's beliefs.

Meanwhile, don't shy away from *sharing* this process with your audience. Early cover reveals, "making-of" blog posts, or short teaser chapters can serve the same function as a well-placed "Act One" in your marketing, igniting curiosity and inviting them to invest in your creative path.

Storytelling is, at its heart, a **dialogue** between artist and audience, between the words you put on the page and the imaginations that bring them to life. By unifying the core techniques of craft with an equally empathetic approach to marketing and reader engagement, you're constructing more than just novels. You're building a **home** for readers to revisit again and again.

We hope the frameworks, examples, and tools in these chapters have equipped you to write stories that don't merely entertain but *connect*—to universal fantasies, to life's pivotal transitions, and ultimately to the vast community of readers searching for a tale that feels like it was written just for them.

If you can deliver that, not once, but consistently, you will have created something truly extraordinary: a bridge between your creative vision and the hearts of those who need it most. Let this be the spark that encourages you to refine your plot, deepen your characters, and, most importantly, continue reaching for that moment when a reader sighs in recognition and says, "*This* is the story I've been waiting for."

Russell Nohelty

WHAT'S NEXT?

It's over!

If you've read this far, I want to thank you for your persistence and perseverance. I know that learning about business isn't any creator's favorite thing to do in the world; however, just by reading this book, you are so much further ahead than most creatives on this planet.

I would say to give yourself a round of applause, but I've worked very hard throughout this book not to be cheesy and don't want to ruin it now.

Well, maybe just a little applause would be okay. Not too long, though, because now the real work begins.

That's right…work.

As much knowledge as I crammed into this book, it's truly just a primer to gear you up for a lifelong pursuit of learning about the business of art. The goal of this book is to give you the necessary tools so you can go out there and build the foundation of a creative career.

It's not an endpoint. It's a beginning.

You made it to the end of this book. Now, you are prepared for the horrible and yet consistent world of late-stage capitalism. However, you still have to live in it.

Write Irresistible Books that Readers Devour

If you loved this book, I hope you go check out *The Author Stack,* my weekly newsletter that goes into even more depth about how to build your creator career.

https://www.theauthorstack.com/

As a paid member, you get access to a ton of my previous work, including fiction, non-fiction, courses, and more.

RESOURCES:

- *How to Build Your Creative Career*
- *How to Become a Successful Author*
- *Advanced Growth Tactics for Authors*
- *Get Your Book Selling on Kickstarter*
- *Get Your Book Selling on Facebook*
- *Get Your Book Selling with Cross-Promotion*
- *Get Your Book Selling at Events and Signings*
- *Get Your Book Selling in Print*
- *The Author Ecosystems*
- *Create Profitable Facebook Ads course*
- *Fund Your Book with Kickstarter course*
- *How to set up and run an awesome anthology course*
- *How to run a viral giveaway to build your mailing list*
- *Write a Great Novel course*
- *How to Build an Audience from Scratch minicourse*
- *10x your productivity course*
- *Lessons and lectures*
- *Interview archive*
- *Complete Creative data archive*
- *Income reports since 2018*
- *Script library*

There's probably even more now since I update it every couple of months.

Russell Nohelty

You can also find my work at: www.russellnohelty.com

Feel free to email me at russell@wannabepress.com and let me know what you think, and please leave a review. The only way I know I should keep writing these kinds of books is from your reviews and kind words.

Find more of my work at my blog:

www.theauthorstack.com

Find all my work at my website:

www.russellnohelty.com

Bookbub:

https://www.bookbub.com/profile/russell-nohelty

www.ingramcontent.com/pod-product-compliance
Lightning Source LLC
Chambersburg PA
CBHW070442090526
44586CB00046B/1645